Improving
Articulation and Voice

Improving
Articulation and Voice

Robert G. King
Eastern Kentucky State College

Eleanor M. DiMichael
Queens College

THE MACMILLAN COMPANY, *New York*
COLLIER-MACMILLAN LIMITED, *London*

Library of Congress catalog card number: 66-20818

THE MACMILLAN COMPANY, NEW YORK
COLLIER-MACMILLAN CANADA, LTD., TORONTO, ONTARIO

Printed in the United States of America

Acknowledgments

No book is the result of the labor of only two persons. We are indebted to many for their help and, although we cannot possibly list them all, we would like to acknowledge our special debt to Dr. Claude Wise, Dr. Harvey Halpern, Professor Joe M. Johnson, Mr. Randall Nolte, and our students.

FOR

Greenup and Hazel King

AND

Nick and Zora Gasparovich

without whom

neither we nor this book

would have come into being

Foreword

FOR SOME time in speech literature there has been a need for a brief but comprehensive book on speech improvement. This book has been written with that need in mind. The first half of the volume presents the theory of sound production and placement and contains numerous fresh exercises for improving articulation. All of the sounds of standard American English are covered, singly and in combinations. The second half discusses those factors that contribute to good voice quality. Exercises are provided to develop the techniques involved in voice production: these skills, in turn, are integrated into meaningful speech.

This volume can be used in many different kinds of courses in speech, including public speaking, oral interpretation, and speech improvement for teachers—courses in which the student's voice and articulation must be improved to better his vocal performance. For such courses it can serve as a supplement to a standard text or as a handbook for students with particular needs. The book can also stand on its own as a text for a course in the improvement of articulation and voice, because the theory and exercises are developed in a sequence readily adaptable to classroom use.

In the organization of this volume the authors first concentrate on articulation. This is a practical arrangement, for articulation skills require careful training with ample auditory feedback, and acuity of auditory feedback needs to be established as early as possible in the course. As the authors point out, correct articulation contributes to balanced vocal resonance, to adequate muscular tension required in healthy voice production, and to effective breathing.

The second half of the book focuses on voice skills, stressing both theory and exercises. The exercises improve general vocal quality and are also helpful in overcoming such specific voice problems as harshness, breathiness, stridency, nasality, and lack of projection. These exercises for articulation and voice have been developed from the authors' extensive experience in teaching courses in speech improvement.

Mrs. DiMichael is a lecturer in speech at Queens College of the City University of New York. Dr. King is a professor of speech and chairman of the department at Eastern Kentucky State College.

ARTHUR C. HASTINGS

Stanford University

Foreword to the Student

You ARE about to begin a difficult but rewarding task—that of improving the way you speak. Do not become discouraged: although the task is not easy, it is not impossible. All your present speech patterns were once learned, and therefore you can learn new ones. Of course, it takes effort to replace old, established habits.

Improvement, which implies desired change developed through experience, depends upon two things—purpose and plan. We assume that you are dissatisfied with some aspects of your speech or that you have been made aware of some speech habits that you would like to change. This handbook is focused on the improvement of those acquired speech patterns as they occur in daily conversation, specifically on the production and usage of voice and on articulation. After intelligent and consistent practice, you should develop a pleasant, colorful, well-modulated, and well-produced voice combined with correct, clear, assimilated articulation. The end result of your efforts should be speech that is acceptable without seeming artificial, precise without sounding pedantic.

As a background for your study, let us review briefly some of the reasons you speak as you do and some obstacles to changing your speech, and then preview the plan for improvement that we will follow.

How You Learned:
Why You Speak As You Do

Students often ask, "Why did I learn to speak this way?" or "Why isn't my natural speech better?" The answer is that speech

is a learned psychomotor skill, and your speech patterns are the
result of many influences. Your native speech proficiency is
molded by your heredity and by many kinds of environment.
Heredity gives you the organic structure with which you speak.
Your environment influences the way you learn to use this organic structure. The section of the country in which you were
born and reared, your family's socioeconomic status, the schools
you attended, your personal relationships with other members
of your family and with your friends, your concept of yourself,
the speech patterns you heard and adopted as models—all these
factors played a great part in shaping your speech. Your production of specific sounds, your pronunciation of words, your choice
of vocabulary, and your patterns of intonation are all the result
of your environment and, perhaps even more important, of your
reactions to that environment. Your sensitivity and receptivity to
the surrounding stimuli determined, to a large extent, your communication habits.

How You May Resist Relearning:
Obstacles to Be Overcome

"If I speak the speech I heard, if I picked up my language
patterns from those around me in early childhood, if this is the
way I speak naturally, why should I bother to change it now?"
This attitude is common and is one of several major obstacles to
speech improvement. Although the objection is common, it is
based on false assumptions. No speech pattern is natural in the
sense of being acquired automatically; all speech is learned. It
follows, then, that you may have learned patterns that are not
the most effective and are not the conventionally accepted patterns. The fact that you learned one set of speech habits *first*
should not deter you from learning another set of speech habits
now.

A second major obstacle to improving your speech with which
you may have to deal is resistance to change rooted in the self-
concept. Your speech is very much a part of you; your speech
patterns were developed partly, as we have noted, because of your

way of thinking of yourself. Any attempt to change your speech may pose some sort of psychological "threat" to you. If so, you will have to face these difficulties and deal with them realistically. One student whom we knew, for example, had very poor voice production and was in danger of serious vocal damage. He resisted changing his faulty production because, he said, it would make him "sound less masculine." Not until his resistance to understanding was faced and the erroneous self-evaluation changed did he improve his speech.

A third major handicap in speech improvement is the fact that you have been practicing your old speech habits for a long time. Constant repetition has reinforced the pattern, and it is deeply ingrained. It will not be easy to replace habits developed early and repeated constantly. But new habits can be introduced, developed, and reinforced. If you are stimulated by a genuine need to improve, if you are motivated by a genuine desire to improve, and if you are activated by a genuine willingness to improve, you *can* overcome the obstacles.

How You May Relearn:
A Plan for Improvement

To replace an old speech habit with a new one requires three steps: (1) awareness of the difficulty, (2) development of new skills, and (3) transference into conversation. Throughout this handbook, we attempt to make you aware of the speech problems which you may need to work on, to tell you simply and clearly how to develop the new skill, and to give you manageable practice materials through which you can establish the new habits and transfer them into your everyday speech.

For the sake of clarity and convenience, this handbook is divided into two sections, but you should not conclude from this division that articulation and voice are unrelated. The fact is that the two are mutually dependent in several respects. Part I, "Articulation," treats speech standards, the production of the sounds of American English, and the combination of these sounds into meaningful speech. Part II, "Voice," concentrates on the physical production of voice and on the effective use of voice. Basic information in anatomy and physiology is presented only to the extent it is needed to clarify effective vocal training. This section stresses the techniques involved in acquiring skills in (1) effective resonance, (2) correct respiration habits, and (3) adequate laryngeal tension. Since resonance is governed to a large extent by the movement of the articulators and by relaxation of the oral and pharyngeal cavities, and since you can develop initial skill in these areas through your work on articulation, Part II begins with work on resonance. This order for the material is distinctive, but it seems to us a logical progression. The work on voice in this handbook is concerned only with those defects which exist in the habitual quality of a speaker. For clinically significant cases of quality disorder, such as hysterical aphonia or nasality following paralysis of the palate, you should consult a speech therapist or a speech clinic.

R. G. K.

E. M. D.

Contents

PART I

Articulation

Articulation Glossary

Affricate A single sound (phoneme) that is, phonetically, a blend of a plosive and a fricative.

Allophone A variant form of a phoneme, which may be used interchangeably with other variants without changing the meaning.

Alveolar ridge The gum ridge behind the upper front teeth.

Articulation Obstruction (either partial or complete) of the air stream by the lips, teeth, tongue, palate, and velum.

Aspiration Release of a sound with a puff of air.

Assimilation A change in a sound caused by the influence of a neighboring sound.

Cognate One of a pair of sounds, articulated in the same place and manner, which are distinguished from each other by the presence or absence of vibration of the vocal folds.

Consonant A speech sound characterized by obstruction, either partial or complete, of the air stream.

Continuant A consonant on which the air stream is impeded but not completely stopped; a sustainable consonant.

Dentalization Distortion of a sound by placing the tongue on or near the teeth.

Devoicing Weakening of vocal vibration on a voiced consonant because of the influence of a neighboring voiceless sound or of the pause following the sound.

Diphthong A blend of two vowels, the first of which is fairly strong and the second of which is relatively weak.

Enunciation Clarity of utterance; precision of articulation.

Fricative A consonant on which the air stream is emitted with

3

4 Articulation*Articulation*

audible friction because the air is forced out between two articulators.

Fronting   Distortion of a sound by arching the tongue near the front of the mouth rather than at the back or center of the mouth.

Glide   A consonant on which the articulators move from one position to another.

Glottis   The space between the vocal folds.

Lateral   The consonant on which the air is emitted over the sides of the tongue.

Lowering   Distortion of a sound by dropping the tongue below its usual position for formation of the sound.

Medializing   Distortion of a sound by arching the tongue in the center of the mouth rather than at the back or front of the mouth.

Nasalization   A distortion caused by nasal resonance on non-nasal sounds.

Nasals   Consonants on which the air is emitted through and resonated in the nose.

Occlusion   The bringing of the edges of the inner surfaces of the upper front teeth and the edges of the outer surfaces of the lower front teeth together.

Phone   (from the Greek φωνή, voice) A sound of the language.

Phoneme   A class or family of sounds (phones) that are phonetically similar and that may be used interchangeably without changing the meaning.

Phonemics   The study of the significantly different sounds (phonemes) of a language.

Phonetics   The study of sounds (phones).

Pronunciation   The utterance of words.

Raising   Distortion of a sound by elevating the tongue from the usual position for forming the sound.

Retracting   Distortion of a sound by placing the tongue back of the usual position for making the sound.

Sibilants   The high-frequency sounds characterized by hissing— / s /, / z /, / ʃ /, / ʒ /.

Stop (Plosive)   A consonant on which the air stream is completely obstructed.

Unvoicing Distortion of a voiced consonant by turning it into its voiceless cognate.

Velum The soft palate.

Vowel A speech sound on which the air stream is relatively unobstructed and which is formed by modification of resonance in the mouth.

CHAPTER 1

Standards and Usage

IF YOU were a French student studying the pronunciation of French in France, you could check your own pronunciation of the language against the standards set by the Academy. In Great Britain, there is also a preferred standard of pronunciation, but it is not laid down by any official agency or organization of scholars. It is the dialect that distinguishes the educated class from the lower social classes. This dialect is known as "Received British Pronunciation" because it is the kind of language characteristic of the people received into the homes of those in the highest social stratum.

If there is no agency to prescribe with authority what is standard pronunciation of American English and if there is not one nationally uniform standard pronunciation that is taught in the influential schools and universities and that distinguishes the upper class, is there such a thing as "standard American English"? If there are acceptable regional variations in pronunciation, can we possibly talk about "standard American English"? To both these questions, the authors answer a definite (but relative) *yes*.

Standard speech, like good manners in general and table manners in particular, is not prescribed by law, codified in any statute, or decreed by any authority. Rather, it consists of socially accepted conventions, established by the practice of the social leaders of our communities who set the style and fashion for most of our practices and the criteria of what is in good taste. You do not have to conform to these patterns unless you want to, but if you want to fit into the social circles of which they are characteristic and in which they are expected, it will probably be necessary for you to "go along."

A young college freshman we know ate everything with a spoon when he came to college. He shoveled the food down, but he digested and assimilated it as well as any of us. If the purpose of eating is simply to get the food into the mouth, then he performed the task with relative efficiency. We must tell you, however, that people noticed that Bob's table practices were quite different from those of everyone else on campus. Bob himself soon became aware of the differences in his eating procedures, too, even though no one said a word to him about them, and he decided to conform to the practices of his new group. Had Bob not changed his eating habits, he probably would not have been ostracized, but he certainly would have been thought odd and he would have limited himself socially and economically.

The purpose of speech is, of course, to communicate, and your first concern should be to communicate as efficiently as possible. But merely being understood may not be enough. There are socially accepted patterns, and one who deviates from them (just as one who is too different in his table manners) is sure to be noticed. And you should recognize that failure to conform to the established speech patterns of cultivated speakers may be a social and economic handicap to you. Whether they should or not, other people judge you on the basis of your speech, and the impression conveyed by your articulation and voice may very greatly influence their total impression of you as a person.

To define what is standard American English is difficult, because in the United States "standard speech" is neither absolute nor uniform. It is the pattern of speech used by the social leaders of your community or area, but because we cannot give an absolute definition of *social leaders* we cannot give an absolute definition of *standard speech*. Instead, "standard speech patterns" are relative—related to the socially accepted conventions of that indefinable but influential group of people who set the standard of style in all areas of life in your community. Nor is "standard speech" uniform throughout the entire United States. Anyone who has traveled in this country and has talked with prominent leaders in different sections of the country recognizes the fact that there are regional variations. These dialectal differences cannot be considered substandard, because they are used by the social leaders in the various areas. There is some variety in standard speech in this country.

Actually, it is much easier to define what is substandard than to describe with accuracy what is standard. Either one or both of the following characteristics marks speech as substandard: (1) that which interferes with communication, and (2) that which calls attention to itself.

Obviously, the principal purpose of speaking is to communicate a message. If the way you speak makes it difficult for you to be understood, whatever causes the difficulty is substandard. "Whajawah?" for "What did you want?" is substandard because it is difficult to understand. The omissions and overassimilations have needlessly complicated the listener's task.

There are, of course, substandardisms that can be understood. The person who says *bekoss* for *because* and *dis, dat, dese,* and *dose* for the demonstrative pronouns communicates his message. Although we understand what he is saying, we note that it is "incorrect" (by which we mean that it is unconventional) and definitely substandard. If attention of the cultivated, discriminating listener is diverted from what is said to the way it is said, from the message to the method of pronunciation, then the pattern is substandard. At this point, we should make one thing absolutely clear. Any pattern that calls attention to itself is substandard. Speech that is careless and slovenly calls attention to itself, but so does speech that is pedantic and perniciously precise, and both are equally substandard. Neither the person who says *solar* for *soldier* nor the person who says *soldyour* is speaking standard American English. Both are failing to conform to the prevailing pattern of contemporary cultivated American usage.

You are aware, of course, that no one always speaks exactly the same way in all situations. You adjust your speech to the situation by selecting the degree of formality appropriate for each particular occasion. Informal speech is not substandard; it is an acceptable variety of standard speech. These variations in your speech patterns are somewhat analogous to those used in your writing. You do not write a personal letter in the same style as an essay or thesis. You do not speak the same way in a conversation in your home as you do on the platform giving a lecture. Choose the form of standard speech (formal or informal) on the basis of propriety.

Summary

Standard American English is relative and varied. It is the pattern used by the social leaders in each community or area; regional variation of itself does not make speech substandard. Patterns that are substandard interfere with communication and call attention to themselves. Informal and formal patterns are acceptable varieties of standard speech, and a speaker of standard American English uses both—selecting for each occasion the appropriate variety.

CHAPTER 2

Sound Production

THIS CHAPTER is concerned with the production of the sounds of American English.

The sounds of the language are classified as consonants, affricates, vowels, and diphthongs. Consonants are speech sounds on which the air column is either stopped completely or markedly impeded in their emission. Affricates are consonant combinations that form a single sound unit; that is, they sound like a single sound, although they are, phonetically, a combination of two consonants. Vowels, in contrast with most consonants, are speech sounds emitted with relatively little obstruction of the air stream; they are comparatively "open" sounds produced by modification of the resonance in the mouth. A diphthong is a blend of two vowels.

Sounds in Isolation

We will consider sounds first in isolation and then in some common combinations. After the explanation of the correct production of each sound or combination, you will find a discussion of the common deviations from standard usage and exercises for practice in improving your own production of the sound.

Consonants

Consonants are classified in terms of (1) the presence or absence of vibration of the vocal folds, (2) the place of articulation of the sound, and (3) the manner of emission of the air stream.

Place of Articulation:

Manner of Emission:	Two Lips (Bilabial)	Lip-Teeth (Labio-Dental)	Tongue-Teeth (Lingua-Dental)	Tongue-Gum Ridge (Lingua-Alveolar)	Tongue Behind Teeth (Lingua-Post-Dental)	Tongue-Palate (Lingua-Palatal)	Tongue-Soft Palate (Lingua-Velar)	Glottis (Glottal)
Stops (Plosives)	p b			t d			k g	ʔ
Continuants Lateral				l				
Nasals				n			ŋ	
Fricatives	ʍ	f v	θ ð		s z	ʃ ʒ		h
Glides	w					j r	(w)	

Note: Voiceless sounds are played to the left of each column; voiced sounds, to the right. Also note that / w / has two articulations: lip-rounding and lingua-velar approximation. Hence, it occurs in two places in the table.

For example, the consonant in the word *be* would be classified as a voiced bilabial stop-plosive, because it is made with the vocal folds vibrating, it is articulated by the two lips, and it is emitted after a complete stoppage of the air stream in a little explosion.

(1) VOCAL VIBRATION. Of the 23 consonants of the English language, 14 are made with the vocal folds vibrating. These sounds are the first consonants in the following words:

/ b /	bare	/ m /	meal
/ d /	dare	/ n /	kneel
/ g /	get	/ ŋ /	angle
/ v /	vet	/ l /	low
/ ð /	then	/ w /	woe
/ z /	Zen	/ r /	rue
/ ʒ /	azure	/ j /	you

There are nine consonants not made with vocal vibration. These consonants are the initial sounds in the following words:

/ p /	pie	/ θ /	thigh
/ t /	tie	/ s /	sigh
/ k /	Chi	/ ʃ /	shy
/ ʌ /	why	/ h /	high
/ f /	fie		

Some of the consonants can be grouped into pairs called cognates. Each of the two sounds in the pair is articulated in the same place and released in the same manner; they differ in that one is voiceless and the other is voiced.

	Voiceless:	*Voiced:*	
peer	/ p /	/ b /	beer
toe	/ t /	/ d /	dough
kill	/ k /	/ g /	gill
whey	/ ʌ /	/ w /	way
fear	/ f /	/ v /	veer
thigh	/ θ /	/ ð /	thy
sue	/ s /	/ z /	zoo
assure	/ ʃ /	/ ʒ /	azure

(2) PLACE OF ARTICULATION. (*See* Figure 2–1.) To form consonants, the air stream is impeded in its emission at some point by the articulators—lips, teeth, tongue, hard palate, and velum (soft palate). If the closure is complete, the sound produced is a stop-plosive; if the closure is partial, the sound is a continuant. To impede the air column and thus articulate a sound, one may bring together the two lips, the lips and teeth, the tongue and teeth, the tongue and gum ridge, the tongue and hard palate, or the tongue and velum. One sound, the / h /, is made by squeezing the air through the vocal folds.

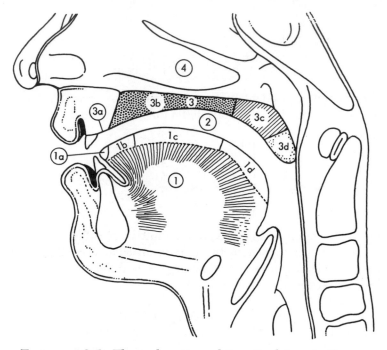

F I G U R E 2–1. The oral cavity and its articulators. 1: Tongue. 1a: Tongue tip. 1b: Blade of tongue. 1c: Front of tongue. 1d: Back of tongue. 2: Mouth (oral) cavity. 3: Palate. 3a: Gum, or alveolar, ridge. 3b: Hard palate. 3c: Soft palate. 3d: Uvula. 4: Nasal cavity. Reprinted with permission of the Macmillan Company from Jon Eisenson, *The Improvement of Voice and Diction,* 2d ed. Copyright © The Macmillan Company, 1965.

(3) MANNER OF EMISSION. Consonants are divided into two groups according to their acoustic characteristics. Stop-plosives are sounds in which two articulators are brought together to stop the air stream completely, and after a build-up of the air pressure, the air is released in a tiny explosion. If the release results in a vigorous puff of air, the stop is *aspirated;* in some instances, stops are released without such a vigorous puff of air and are said to be *unaspirated* or *imploded.* There are six stop-plosives in English, and a seventh called the glottal stop is heard as a substandard form when substituted for another stop. Continuants, unlike plosives, can be sustained; they are sounds that can be continued, because the air stream is impeded (but not stopped) and squeezed between two articulators. Continuants are subdivided into four groups of sounds: (1) the lateral, which is emitted with the air coming over the sides of the tongue; (2) nasals, which are emitted with nasal resonance; (3) fricatives, which are friction noises; and (4) the glides, in which the articulators move from one position to another.

STOP-PLOSIVES

/ p /　and　/ b /

If you raise the velum so that no air can escape through the nose, block the air stream by closing the two lips, and then release the compressed air by quickly opening the lips, you will produce a bilabial plosive. There are two bilabial stop-plosives in English: one is voiceless, represented by / p /, and one is voiced, represented by / b /.

There are three common deviations or distortions of these two sounds: (1) incomplete closure, (2) overaspiration, and (3) unvoicing.

Incomplete closure of the articulators on plosive sounds results in slovenly, indistinct speech. The air stream must be *stopped* to form stop-plosives! Have you ever heard a careless speaker pronounce the word *obvious* without quite closing the two lips completely to form the / b /? Check to make sure that your stop is complete on such words as *capful, subvert,* and *obverse.*

Overaspiration is another common distortion of / p / and / b /. Although the amount of aspiration on these consonants varies, depending upon the position of the sound in the syllable and upon the sound which precedes or follows, one must be careful not to overexplode / p / or / b /.

Before voiceless sounds and as the final sound in a phrase, / b / may be slightly devoiced. It should not, however, be completely unvoiced. The word *tribe*, for example, should certainly not sound like *tripe*, and *Abe* should not be turned into *ape*.

Materials for Practicing / p / and / b /

peat	beat	happy	abbey	sop	sob
pin	bin	rupee	Ruby	cup	cub
pay	bay	dappled	dabbled	rope	robe
peg	beg	appeal	Abeel	rip	rib
pad	bad	crumple	crumble	gap	gab
pole	bowl	ample	amble	cop	cob
poor	boor	Harpur	harbor	crap	crab
pump	bump	staple	stable	lope	lobe

1. Never buy a pig in a poke.
2. He played basketball for a private school.
3. I got into trouble by leaping and ripping the tapestry.
4. Mr. Blake was probably disturbed by that shibboleth.
5. Perry has been stationed at an army post near Budapest, Alabama.
6. Except for a couple of brilliant cab drivers, no one has ever robbed me.
7. The symbolism in the play is far from simple.
8. No one is ever absolutely beyond help.
9. Our president was quite unhappy over the bad publicity we received.
10. Don't punctuate your sentences with great bursts of air on the plosive sounds.

/ t /   and   / d /

If you raise the velum to prevent the air from escaping through the nose, block the air stream at the front by pressing the tip of the tongue against the gum ridge, and then release the air by quickly dropping the tongue tip, you will produce a lingua-alveolar stop-plosive. There are two such stops in English: / t / which is voiceless and / d / which is voiced. In making these sounds, you must be careful to narrow the tongue to a sharp point, to press the tongue tip firmly against the gum ridge, and to make the release quick. (See Figure 2–2.)

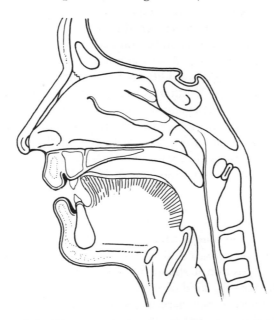

FIGURE 2–2. Diagram of the mouth, showing contact point for / t /, / d /, and / l /. Essentially the same tongue tip and gum ridge contact is made for the / n /. The / n /, however, is produced with a relaxed and lowered soft palate. Reprinted with permission of The Macmillan Company from Jon Eisenson and Paul H. Boase, *Basic Speech*, 2d ed. Copyright © The Macmillan Company, 1950, 1964.

There are three common deviations of these sounds: (1) incomplete closure, (2) dentalization, and (3) unvoicing.

The sound represented by / t / in the words *tub, stub, butter,* and *but* all differ in the amount of aspiration on their release, but they are alike in that they are all complete closures. The tongue tip must touch the gum ridge and check the air stream for an instant. In the same way, the sound represented by / d / in the words *dub, budding,* and *bud* differ slightly in the amount of aspiration on release, but they do not differ in the completeness of the closure. Failure to block the air column on these stops is characteristic of careless, slovenly speech.

Another deviation is dentalization, the placing of the tongue on or near the teeth rather than on the gum ridge. Although / t / and / d / are made acceptably on the teeth before the two *th* sounds in English (the / d / in *width* and *breadth,* for example, and the / t / in *eighth* and *hit the ball* are dental), dentalization of / t / and / d / in other contexts distorts the sounds. This change in tongue placement gives a fricative quality to a sound which was intended to be plosive. The resulting / t / sounds a bit like /ts /, and the / d / sounds something like / dz /. Check to be certain that when you make the / t / and / d / your tongue tip goes to the gum ridge, about a quarter of an inch behind the teeth. Pluck that point with your tongue tip. / t / and / d / should be quick, firm clicks—not prolonged, breathy explosions.

Like / b /, the voiced sound / d / may be slightly devoiced before voiceless sounds and as the final sound in a phrase, but even in final position it should not be completely unvoiced. You should not make the kind of mistake made by one of our students who read aloud to her class about a horse who was to be *shot* when the author had written about a horse who was to be *shod!*

Materials for Practicing / t / and / d /

dear	tear	shudder	shutter	aid	ate
den	ten	medal	metal	bud	but
dapper	tapper	plodding	plotting	bad	bat
dot	tot	ladder	latter	heard	hurt
doubt	tout	bidder	bitter	node	note
daunt	taunt	ruder	rooter	Swede	sweet
dub	tub	herding	hurting	loud	lout
dame	tame	contended	contented	tied	tight

1. The Transit Authority pressed him into an untenable position.
2. One should do his best, even in an unimportant speech.
3. The priest recommended an hour of meditation every day.
4. Are hereditary factors or environmental factors more important in developing personality?
5. According to the teacher, improvement will depend on interest, effort, and practice.
6. There is no substitute for drill to develop precise articulation.
7. I took the achievement test, but I didn't do well on it.
8. "Liberty, equality, and fraternity" was a revolutionary motto.
9. The speaker developed a devastating analysis of the current trend.
10. What lawyer today would talk about "the quality of mercy"?
11. Should prostitution be legalized in the United States? I don't think so.
12. The plaintiff demanded restitution, but he didn't get it.
13. The rules on substitutions are not consistent.

/ n /, / l /, / d /, and / t / are all made on the gum ridge. If you have a problem with dentalizing these sounds, be careful to place the tongue tip in the proper place as you read the words across the line. The tongue tip should go to the same spot to make all four initial sounds.

nigh	lie	die	tie
know	low	dough	toe
nip	lip	dip	tip
nor	lore	door	tore
napper	lapper	dapper	tapper
not	lot	dot	tot
nil	Lil	dill	till
nick	lick	Dick	tick
knee	lee	D.	tee
near	leer	dear	tear
numb	Lum	dumb	Tum
gnu	lieu	do	too
nab	lab	dab	tab
Nome	loam	dome	tome
noon	loon	dune	tune
ne'er	lair	dare	tare

1. Touch the tip of the tongue to the alveolar ridge.
2. Do not explode it; tap it.
3. The tendency to dentalize the / t / and / d / is not too unusual in New York City.
4. Do not let the tongue tip slide forward.
5. We do not want a nuclear explosion. Cut down on the fall-out.
6. Do not touch the teeth on the / t / sound.
7. It will be necessary to practice until proper placement feels natural.
8. One must undo an old habit and replace it with a new one.
9. Let nothing deter you.
10. Do not limit your practice to laboratory sessions.
11. No one else will be able to establish new speech patterns for you.
12. Whenever you talk, try to do your best.
13. Listen carefully and critically to your own speech.
14. Learn to control the release of the air efficiently.
15. Make clear articulation a habit.

Work for Clear, Firm Stops:

1. I shudder every time I think about it.
2. We prefer shutters at the windows.

3. We are plodding along, but progress should be faster.
4. Malcontents were plotting against the authorities.

5. That old house needs a protective coating of paint.
6. Coding messages is an interesting but difficult task.

7. I hate to be patted on the head.
8. You ought to be put in a padded cell.

9. Puritans were particular about what puddings they would eat.
10. I'm putting this episode into your permanent record.

11. The student pleaded with the instructor to change the grade.
12. Pleated trousers are a relatively recent innovation.

13. Adam had marital problems, too.
14. We live in the shadow of the atom bomb.

15. It really wasn't nearly as bad as I expected it to be.
16. She broke the baseball bat over his head.

17. It was an effort, but we weighed her.
18. Waiter, will you bring me the check?

19. Today one should bet on a mudder.
20. That is no reason for him to mutter constantly.

21. I plan to audit the course.
22. Ought it to take much time?

23. I don't think I can mend it.
24. I told him I meant it.

25. The artist bowed in response to the tumultuous ovation.
26. It will be his last bout in the Garden.

/ k / and / g /

If you block the air stream by pressing the back of the tongue against the soft palate while the velum is raised, and then release the compressed air quickly by dropping the tongue from the soft palate, you will produce a lingua-velar stop-plosive. There are two lingua-velar stops in English: one that is voiceless, represented by / k /, and one that is voiced, represented by / g /.

There are three common distortions related to these two sounds: (1) incomplete closure, (2) overaspiration, and (3) unvoicing.

As in the case of the other stops, it is necessary to check the air stream completely on / k / and / g /. Careless speakers pronounce such words as *acceptable, accede,* and *succulent* without quite making a complete stop on the / k / and you may have noted that some people do not fully close the / g / in such words as *ignition* and *recognize*.

Like other stop-plosives, / k / and / g / vary in the amount of aspiration upon release: like the other plosives also, / k / and / g / can be overaspirated. Be careful, especially on the voiceless plosives, not to release too great a puff of air.

Before voiceless sounds and when final in a phrase, / g / is slightly devoiced, but should never be completely unvoiced. Even when it is the last word in the sentence, *lug* should not sound like *luck* or *stag* like *stack*.

Materials for Practicing / k / and / g /

Kaye	gay	meeker	meager	lock	log
coast	ghost	racket	ragged	back	bag
cause	gauze	anchor	anger	Rick	rig
crime	grime	lacquered	laggard	muck	mug
crape	grape	Becker	begger	Beck	beg
crypt	gripped	ankle	angle	leak	league
clue	glue	backing	bagging	hawk	hog
class	glass	pokey	pogy	hack	hag
clean	glean	bucking	bugging	luck	lug

1. The Clarks have a cottage and garden in the country.
2. A government employee, he still kept his membership in the key club.
3. The crowd found the combat gripping, but the combatants themselves were cool and calculating.
4. Every society has its own golden calf. Is ours success?
5. He is not an ignorant man, but he did not recognize the governor.
6. In such a struggle, there is rarely a victor; one must be rugged and clever merely to survive.
7. Above being a common crook, a smuggler is a racketeer and a rogue.
8. To prevent students from haggling over exam grades, some professors keep all questions exceptionally vague.
9. Actually, I cannot accede to your request, since I would be an accessory to your crime.

/ ? /

The glottis is the space between the vocal folds. A sound articulated at the vocal folds is, therefore, called a glottal sound; a stop-plosive formed by closing the vocal folds, building up the air pressure, and then releasing the air in a plosion is called a glottal stop. Such a popping sound occurs as an accepted speech sound in a number of other languages. Though it is heard in the speech of English speakers, it is not a sound of standard American English. It is most likely to occur in two places: (1) before initial vowels in a syllable, and (2) as a substitute for the lingua-alveolar plosive in / tl / and / tn / combinations. The correct formation of / tl / and / tn / will be discussed elsewhere (see page 90), but check to see if you use a glottal stop in the following words and phrases. You should be able to initiate the vowels without a shock or pop of air at the vocal folds.

Pronounce the following words, avoiding a glottal stop at the places (marked by asterisks) where it is likely to be inserted:

*oh * oh
cha*otic
hi*atus
*I did
the *eyes
a*orta
co*ordinate
*O *Athenians

CONTINUANTS

The Lateral

/ 1 /

There is only one lateral consonant sound in English, represented by / 1 /. To form the sound, the tongue tip is raised to
the gum ridge, and the air passes over the sides of the tongue
out of the mouth, the velum being closed. Like / t / and / d /,
the / 1 / is a lingua-alveolar sound.

There are two forms, or allophones, of the / 1 / sound: the
light / 1 /, which occurs initially in a syllable or after an initial
consonant before front vowels, and *dark* / ł /, which occurs in
initial position before back vowels, in final position, and before
final consonants. A *light* / 1 / would occur, then, in the words
lean and *glean;* a *dark* / ł / would occur in *lewd, glued, hell,*
and *help.* The difference in acoustic quality between the *light*
/ 1 / and *dark* / ł / is caused by a difference in the position of
the back of the tongue; the back of the tongue is raised toward
the soft palate on the *dark* / ł /. The position of the tip of the
tongue is the same on both forms of / 1 /. After voiceless sounds,
/ 1 / is slightly devoiced. There is slight devoicing of the / 1 /
in the words *play, clay, flay,* and *slay,* for example.

There are four common distortions of the / 1 /: (1) slack articulation, (2) confusion of *dark and light* / 1 /, (3) dentalization, and (4) labialization.

You have doubtless heard a speaker whose / 1 / sound, especially in the middle of words, was not distinct. It is quite likely that the speaker was simply not touching the gum ridge with the tongue tip to form the sound. Check to be certain that your tongue tip presses against the ridge on the / 1 / in such words as *relevant, challenge, tranquillity, quality,* and *analysis.* In the South, there is another common distortion of the / 1 /. In words where the / 1 / precedes the final consonant, failure to touch the gum ridge with the tongue tip on the / 1 / sound may result in its sounding more like / ʊ / (the vowel in the word *took*) or / ə / (the first vowel in the word *above*) than like an / 1 /. The word *help*, then, would become [hɛʊp] or [hɛəp], which are clearly substandard.

Confusion with regard to the *light and dark* / 1 / is another problem sometimes associated with this sound. Some speakers for whom English is a second language always use the *light* / 1 / no matter where the sound occurs. They could correct this element of a foreign accent by becoming aware that there are two forms of the sound, that they are made with the back of the tongue in a slightly different position, and that the two allophones have different acoustic qualities. Some native speakers of American English also confuse the two forms by using the *dark* / ɫ / in all positions.

When an / 1 / sound precedes either the voiced *th* or voiceless *th* sounds, the / 1 / will be made with the tongue on the teeth. The / 1 / in the word *stealth*, for example, would be dental. But dentalization of the / 1 / except before the *th* sounds is a distortion. Check to be certain that when you make the / 1 / you do not put the tongue on the upper teeth or between the teeth.

If lip movement is substituted for tongue movement in the formation of the / 1 /—that is, if you do not lift your tongue tip to the gum ridge but instead raise the back of the tongue and purse your lips as if for / u / (the vowel in *boot*) or / w /— then you are said to labialize the / 1 / sound. This distortion is associated with "baby talk" and you should practice to get your tongue moving to the proper spot to make the sound.

Materials for Practicing / l /

led	teller	dell
lip	pillow	pill
leave	velar	veal
Luke	cooling	cool
late	tailor	tail
loaf	Foley	foal
log	galling	gall
lug	gullet	gull
lame	melee	mail
limb	miller	mill

1. Let me call you sweetheart. You call everybody darling.
2. I'll sell it to you for a dollar.
3. Don't be silly. Of course, I'm willing.
4. Most lovers think jealousy should be a felony.
5. She knelt at the altar rail.
6. As the ball sailed between the goal posts, the team set a field goal record.
7. The Long Island Railroad is asking for help from the federal government.
8. Leonard has failed the oral examination again.
9. We'll sail for Europe on the first of April.
10. It is a delicate matter to expose a friend's fallacy.
11. Are all the lectures in this college dull?
12. No one told me there were so many scholarships available.
13. Sally belongs to a mutual admiration society.
14. You can't pull the wool over my eyes.
15. Why do you like to study the fraternity files?

The Nasals

/ m /   / n /   and   / ŋ /

There are three nasal continuant consonants in English. All are made by blocking the air stream at some point in the mouth while the velum is lowered, permitting emission of the air through and resonation in the nose. Each of the nasal sounds is articulated at the place of articulation of one of the pairs of stop-plosives: the bilabial nasal / m / is articulated by the two lips, as are / p / and / b /; the lingua-alveolar nasal / n / is articulated with the tip of the tongue on the gum ridge, as are / t / and / d /; and the lingua-velar nasal / ŋ / is articulated with the back of the tongue against the soft palate, as are / k / and / g /. (*See* Figure 2–3.)

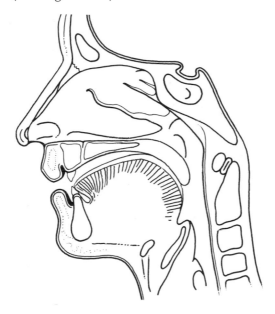

F I G U R E 2–3. Articulatory adjustments for [ŋ]. Note relaxed (lowered) soft palate. Reprinted with permission of The Macmillan Company from Jon Eisenson, *The Improvement of Voice and Diction,* 2d ed. Copyright © The Macmillan Company, 1965.

All three nasals are voiced sounds, although they are slightly devoiced before or after voiceless sounds in the same syllable.

There are six common problems associated with the nasal sounds: (1) denasality, (2) severe nasality on adjacent vowels, (3) substitution of a nasalized vowel for a vowel plus nasal consonant, (4) dentalization of / n /, (5) substitution of / n / for final / ŋ /, and (6) / ŋ / confusion.

The lack of adequate nasal resonance on the three nasal sounds is called denasality. It is a cold-in-the-head quality, and may result from colds, adenoids, or some other obstruction of the nasal resonator or from faulty speech habits. The nasals are long, resonant, "humming" continuants; full nasal resonance is needed for brilliant tone and good projection. If you have a problem with denasality, you should consult a doctor and a speech therapist. On your own, you can work to give adequate duration (nasals are two-beat sounds) and full resonance in the nose on the / m /, / n /, and / ŋ /.

Slight nasalization of vowels adjacent to nasal sounds is inevitable, but excessive nasalization of these vowels is undesirable. If a vowel precedes a nasal sound, the velum will be lowered while the vowel is still being uttered. If, however, most or all of the vowel (an oral sound, you will remember) is uttered with the velum lowered and the air stream escaping in part through the nose, the sound becomes quite unpleasant. The vowels and diphthongs which seem to offer the greatest temptation toward nasalization are / ɛ /, / æ /, / eɪ /, / aɪ /, and / aʊ /. Check your own pronunciation of such words as *ten, Ann, aim, sign,* and *crown.* Compare the way you say the vowel in *ten* with the way you say the vowel in *Ted.* There should not be a great difference. Make them as much alike as you can. Then compare your pronunciation of *Ann* with *add, aim* with *Abe, sign* with *side,* and *crown* with *crowd.* You must train yourself to direct the air consciously through the mouth or through the nose. The word *how,* for example, since it contains no nasal sounds, should have no nasal resonance, and no air should come through the nose while pronouncing it. You could hold your nose, then, and the pronunciation of the word should not be affected. As a further check, pronounce the word *how* with no nasal emission of air, and then pronounce / nd / with full nasal resonance. Now try the word all together—*hound*—with as little nasality on the diphthong as you can achieve (make it as much like *how* as you can) and as much full nasal resonance on the / n / as you can muster. Work for good resonance in the nasal cavity on the nasal sounds and for as little nasality on the adjacent vowels and diphthongs as possible.

When a vowel or diphthong is followed by a nasal consonant, some speakers drop the nasal consonant altogether and simply nasalize the vowel or diphthong. This substitution of one nasalized vowel or diphthong for both an oral sound plus a nasal consonant is a mark of very careless speech in our language. Nasalized vowels are characteristic of French and Portuguese, but they should be avoided in English. Check your own pronunciation of each of the following words or phrases to be certain that you get good nasal consonants, but no nasalized vowels, in each: *unfurled, unveiled, suntan, one time, emphatic, comfortable, triumvirate.*

Speakers who tend to dentalize / t /, / d /, and / l / in all positions often dentalize the / n / as well. Like / t /, / d /, and / l /, the /n / will be made on the teeth when it occurs before one of the *th* sounds, as in *tenth* and *on the teeth.* In all other positions, however, the / n / should be made on the gum ridge.

In informal speech situations, especially in the South, many cultivated speakers use "in" in place of "ing" in such words as *coming* and *going.* The / ɪŋ / is still preferred, however, and we would encourage you to use it.

Some people who have learned English as a second language and many speakers in the metropolitan New York area demonstrate confusion on the use of the / ŋ / sound. There seem to be two sources of confusion with regard to this sound. One is the influence of a language which does not include the pronunciation of both / ŋ / and / ŋg /. The other is spelling, which contributes to the confusion because, though / ŋ / is a single sound, it is usually represented in our spelling by the two letters *n* and *g.* It is also sometimes spelled *ngue* (in words like *meringue* and *tongue*) and in other words is represented by the single letter *n* (as in words like *blink* and *bank*).

If you have a problem with this sound, you should note the generalizations about its pronunciation that follow.

1. When a word ends in the spelling *ng* or *ngue,* the word ends in the single nasal consonant / ŋ /. No / g / or / k / is ever

sounded in these words, even if the next word begins with a vowel. The addition of the extra sound is considered substandard. Check your own pronunciation of *sing it, hang on,* and *calling all cars* to be certain that you do not add / k / or / g / after the nasal sound.

2. When you add a word-forming suffix to a word which ends in *ng* or *ngue,* there is usually no / g /. When the *ng* spelling is in the middle of a word and you can divide the word into a root word ending in *ng* and a suffix, the *ng* represents the one sound / ŋ /. *Singer,* for example, can be divided into the root *sing* and its suffix *er.* There is, therefore, no / g /. In the word *finger,* on the other hand, there is a / g / after the medial / ŋ / because the word cannot be divided into root and suffix. Compare the word *singer* and *single.* The first, as we have noted, has no / g /, but the second is pronounced with / ŋg / because it is not based on the root *sing.* Check your own pronunciation of the words *kingly, longing, hanger, swinger, strongly, haranguing,* and *slangy* to be certain that you do not insert a / g / or / k / after the nasal sound.

There are two groups of exceptions to the principle we have just explained. The comparative and superlative forms of the adjectives *long, strong,* and *young* are all pronounced with / ŋg /. *Longer, stronger, younger, longest, strongest,* and *youngest* contain / g / after the / ŋ /. The second set of exceptions to this principle involves those words formed by adding *ate, ation,* or *al.* Such words as *elongate, prolongation,* and *diphthongal* are pronounced with / ŋg /.

3. When *ng* occurs in the middle of a word and is followed by sounds that do not constitute a word-forming suffix, the word will be pronounced with / ŋg /. *Linger, finger, anger, language, English, singular, single, distinguish,* and *angular* are all examples of this generalization.

You should be aware of two exceptions to this third / ŋ / principle. The word *gingham,* though it cannot be divided into root and suffix, does not contain a / g /. You should also note that the words *length, strength, lengthen,* and *strengthen* are pronounced either with / ŋ / or / ŋk /. Whether you pronounce these words with a / k / or not, be careful not to substitute

/ n / for / ŋ /. This substandard pronunciation, *strength* for *strength,* is more common in the South than elsewhere, but it is heard in other parts of the country as well. You should avoid it. (*See* Figure 2–3.)

Materials for Practicing the Nasals
/ m / and / n /

might	time	need	dean
mead	deem	knit	tin
mate	tame	Ned	den
mat	tam	gnat	tan
mode	dome	note	tone
mud	dumb	nut	ton
moot	tomb	nude	dune

1. My Mary's asleep by the murmuring stream.
2. My name is Ozymandias, king of kings.
3. The noise of the shouting crowd drowned out the music.
4. Some of the students are visions, and others are sights.
5. Who could be lonely with wind and rain for companions?
6. There must always be time to dream.
7. In any case, we must uphold the constitution.
8. There is only temporary comfort in self-deception.
9. Frankly, I found all the nonsense infuriating.
10. Ann works downtown for a venerable institution.
11. Even though he is handsome, they should not have chosen that madman to lead the college band.
12. Mr. Brown, an inveterate traveler, has found a place in the mountains.
13. Many observers are unimpressed by that kind of maneuvering.
14. I'm going out for the tiddlywinks team.
15. The candidates, Tweedledum and Tweedledee, have begun to resort to name-calling.
16. The nasal consonants should be given full nasal resonance on their emission.

/ ŋ /

(Remember that some words contain / ŋ / and some / ŋg /.)

sing	singer
long	longer
hang	hanging
young	youngest
king	kingly
strong	stronger

1. Sing a song of six pence.
2. His youngest brother is studying to be a con man.
3. Staying in training seems to be difficult.
4. Do you go swimming often?
5. Seeing Ann isn't so easy since she moved to Long Island.
6. After finding out the questions, I still gave the wrong answers.
7. I'm remaining in town for the holidays.
8. As long as you are coming anyway, bring it with you.
9. I haven't the strength to swim the length of the pool.
10. There was a long line of men standing at the gate.
11. She can never seem to hang up the phone.
12. Is there a single standard for judging all entrants?
13. "Younger Than Springtime" is a beautiful song.
14. He's been working on all the angles.
15. Mr. Cunningham has been laughing all through the performance.
16. Running away is no answer to one's problems.
17. Practicing every day is necessary for improving your language habits.
18. Did you know that some people elongate diphthongs into triphthongal glides?

Fricatives...

/ ʍ /

If you pucker the lips, raise the back of the tongue toward the velum, and let the tip of the tongue rest against the lower teeth, while you emit the air in a friction type of noise without the vocal folds vibrating, you will produce a voiceless bilabial fricative. In the speech of most speakers of American English, this is the initial sound in words beginning with the spelling *wh* (except, of course, for the words *who, whose, whom, whole, whore, whoop,* and the words formed from them—which begin with / h /). The / ʍ / could be thought of as the voiceless counterpart of / w / and sounds like an *hw* combination, except that it has no voicing.

In some parts of the East, especially in New York City, the / ʍ / sound is rarely used and the / w / is regularly used in its place on the *wh* words. In those areas, the substitution of / w / cannot be called substandard since the majority of educated speakers use it. There is no doubt, though, that the / ʍ / is used by most educated speakers over most of the country. We recommend not using / w / in these words, simply because it results in so many homophones (words which sound alike but differ in spelling and meaning). Check your own pronunciation of the following pairs of words:

what	Watt
whine	wine
where	wear
whale	wail
why	Y
whet	wet
wheel	weal
which	witch
whey	way
white	wight
whit	wit
whirled	world
while	wile
whether	weather
Whig	wig

/ f /   and   / v /

If you bring the upper teeth and the lower lip together and force the air stream out between these two articulators without the vocal folds vibrating, you will produce a voiceless labio-dental fricative, represented by / f /. If you articulate the sound in the same way but allow the vocal folds to vibrate, you will produce a voiced labio-dental fricative, represented by / v /.

There are three problems associated with these consonants which you should be on guard against: (1) omission, (2) unvoicing, and (3) slack articulation.

Both / f / and / v / are rather weak sounds, and you should be careful not to omit them. The temptation will be greatest when the sound is final in a word. You may have had somebody tell you, for example, that he had only "fie dollars." Fie, indeed!

Another common problem associated with these sounds is that of unvoicing the final / v /. All speakers devoice / v / slightly when it precedes a voiceless sound or when it occurs at the end of a phrase or sentence, but the sound should not be completely unvoiced. *Save* should not become *safe,* for example, and *have* should not sound like *half.*

A final distortion of the labio-dental fricatives results from slack articulation. Some careless speakers fail to bring the lower lip up to the teeth to make the sound and therefore substitute a bilabial fricative in place of the / f / or / v /.

Materials for Practicing / f /   and   / v /

fie	five	safe	save
shells	shelves	strife	strive
cars	carves	proof	prove
lies	lives [n.]	life	live [adj.]
rose	roves	leaf	leave
lees	leaves	serf	serve
whose	hooves	belief	believe
does	doves	waif	wave

1. *Twelfth Night* is one of my favorite plays.
2. I will not move; I am not the driver.
3. Save your money. The raffle is fixed.
4. It was hanging above the door for over five days.
5. He could have proved himself a live wire.
6. Mardi Gras is one last carefree fling before pleasures are shelved.
7. A fifth of a cupful is quite enough.
8. I've left the cover of the manuscript at home.
9. Mother always laughs while Father carves the fowl.
10. She forgot and sang the same verse twice.
11. Leaving nothing to the imagination, the devil made the offer quite obvious.
12. It is very foolish to strive against overpowering odds.
13. Would you be very comfortable at a rendezvous with a rival?
14. Somewhat given to violence, that fraternity is called the "home of the brave."

/ θ / and / ð /

If you bring the upper teeth and the blade of your tongue together and let the air ooze out between, you will produce a lingua-dental fricative. The tongue may be placed either against the inside surfaces of the upper front teeth or beneath the edges of the upper front teeth. There are two such sounds in English: one on which the vocal folds do not vibrate, represented by / θ /, and one on which the vocal folds do vibrate, represented by / ð /. Both sounds are represented in our spelling system by *th*, and you cannot tell by the spelling whether to use the voiceless or the voiced sound.

There are three common distortions related to these sounds: (1) raising the tongue behind the teeth, (2) omission, and (3) unvoicing.

Raising the tongue behind the teeth on the production of the two *th* sounds produces a distortion which to the untrained ear

sounds like the substitution of / t / for / θ / and / d / for / ð /.
Those who raise the tongue up on the inner surfaces of the upper
teeth are thought to say *"dis, dat, dese,* and *dose,"* "Come wit
me," "I'll go witcha," and "Nuttin' doin'." If the tongue is not
placed at the bottom of the upper teeth, the sounds will be distorted. Check your own pronunciation of words like *thigh* and
thy, ether and *either, sheath* and *sheathe.*

When the *th* sounds occur in consonant combinations, speakers
who are a bit careless tend to omit them. You should be certain
that you do not say *"What's at?"* for *"What's that?" breed* for
breathed, force for *fourths, links* for *lengths, breeze* for *breathes,*
or *rim* for *rhythm.*

Although the / ð / will be slightly devoiced before voiceless
sounds and when it is the last sound in a phrase, it should never
be completely unvoiced. *Soothe* should never be turned into
sooth, for example, and *teethe* should never become *teeth.*

Materials for Practicing / ð / and / θ /

/ ð /   the, this, that, these, those, then, they, their, them, though,
        then, there, therefore, thereafter

        either, mother, father, bother, farther, other, breathing,
        feather, rather, gather, soothing, smoother, smother,
        leather, heathen, further, bathing, southern, northern

        bathe, clothe, breathe, lathe, soothe, mouth (v.), teethe,
        writhe

/ θ /   thank, thief, thick, think, thin, theme, thesis, thirty,
        theology, thud, thyroid, throb, thrust, throat, throng,
        threw, thrill, thrifty, three, throne

        author, ether, ethics, breathy, Gothic, Athens, Martha,
        mythical, nothing, method, Elizabethan, frothy, earthy

        breath, booth, birth, broth, bath, death, both, earth,
        tooth, forth, myth, moth, mouth, south, north, cloth,
        truth, health, month, ninth, width, length, wealth, worth

/ ð / and / θ /

thy	thigh
then	thin
either	ether
mouth (v.)	mouth (n.)
soothe	sooth
wreathe	wreath

1. They are planning to go home for Thanksgiving.
2. Was that the brand that you ordered?
3. The Crofts are going to the theater tonight.
4. I want to thank you for suggesting a title for my theme.
5. I don't think it fair that the instructor allowed them three extra days on the assignment.
6. We know nothing about the authorship of the material in our files.
7. I'm leaving for Athens in the morning.
8. There's a wealth of information on both topics.
9. Three fifths of the students who responded to the survey admitted that they had cheated.
10. "Is this the face that launched a thousand ships?"
11. Even if it doesn't ruin them, it will cause them a lot of trouble.
12. I live on the South Side, but I'm going to move on Thursday.
13. I'd rather associate with someone who bathes regularly.
14. We got eight thousand answers to the ad, and only five thousand of them were threatening.
15. The Egyptian dancer writhed for an hour but stayed fully clothed.
16. Although we sat there through the whole lecture, none of us accepted his theories.
17. Soothing irate professors is a hard thing to do.
18. One sometimes finds that he must further his career by telling a few half-truths.
19. There are many paths to success—all of them crooked.
20. Both of them in the experiment went to great lengths to continue to breathe.

/ s /   and   / z /

If you occlude the front upper and lower teeth, lightly touch the tongue tip against either the upper or lower gum ridge, and shoot the air stream out of the grooved tongue over the tongue tip and between the front teeth, you will produce a lingua-post-dental fricative. There are two such fricatives in English: one that is voiceless, represented by / s /, and one that is voiced, represented by / z /. Most people articulate these sounds with the tongue behind the upper teeth near the gum ridge rather than behind the lower teeth, but the sounds can be made satis-factorily in either position. In combination with other sounds which are made on the gum ridge (such as / t /, / d /, / l /, and / n /) the sounds are, of course, made in the alveolar posi-tion.

/ s / and / z / are high-frequency noises (the whole family of hissing sounds is called the sibilants) and are not too pleasant at best. Distortions of these sounds, known as lisps, are rather common and quite noticeable. The / s / should be short and sharp (but not whistled), and the / z / should be voiced and correctly articulated.

Although there are a number of other distortions of these sounds, there are seven deviations which are most common: (1) the inter-dental lisp, (2) the dental lisp, (3) the lateral lisp, (4) the whistle, (5) the overaspirated or "noisy" / s / and / z /, (6) lack of adequate aspiration and friction, and (7) un-voicing of the / z /.

The inter-dental distortion of the / s / and / z / is the one commonly thought of as "the lisp." The tongue is thrust out be-tween the teeth so that these sibilants resemble the *th* sounds. If you have an inter-dental lisp, you will have to work to replace your present habit with correct placement of the tongue. *Sing* should not sound like *thing!*

The dental lisp results from incorrect placement of the tongue tip on the teeth. If you have discovered that you tend to dentalize the alveolar consonants / t /, / d /, / l /, / n /, check to see if you also dentalize the / s / and / z /. If you do place the tongue on the teeth, the sound will be distorted.

The lateral lisp is that sound deviation in which the air comes over the sides of the tongue rather than through the center over the tongue tip. It can be the result of pointing the tongue tip toward the alveolar ridge and failing to tense the sides of the tongue against the sides of the hard palate or against the inner surfaces of the side teeth. The air, therefore, escapes over the sides, similar to the production of a correct / 1 / sound. To correct this distortion, (1) place the tongue tip firmly against either gum ridge; (2) occlude the front teeth to assist in focusing the breath over the top of the tongue tip and out through the center of the mouth; (3) seal off the air on each side with the sides of the tongue.

As we noted earlier, the sibilants are high-frequency sounds, but the / s / and / z / should not "whistle." Usually this deviation results from too much tension of the tongue; it may be that you are pressing the tongue tip *too* firmly against the gum ridge. Just relaxing the tongue slightly may correct the whistling noise.

If you make the sounds on the upper ridge, it may be that you are pulling the tongue too far back in the mouth; if so, pull the tongue up a little closer to the teeth (but not on them) to correct this distortion. If you make the sound on the bottom ridge, your tongue tip may be too high—that is, too near the lower teeth; if so, lower the tongue slightly to correct the distortion.

The overaspirated or "noisy" / s / and / z / result from pushing too much air through on the sounds and from prolonging the sounds, if you ssssssssee what we mean. / z /, of course, should be given its proper duration in final position in a word, but / s / is never a long sound. Move on to the sound which follows. In a phrase like "The grass is green," for example, you should practice *the-gra-siz-green*, getting off the / s / quickly and getting on to the next sound.

Although some speakers push through too much air on / s / and / z / and so produce overaspirated sounds, other speakers fail to emit enough air on the sounds so that they not only lack friction, they are almost inaudible. If this is your problem, work for adequate tension of the tongue and an adequate pressure of air.

Although the / z / will be devoiced slightly before voiceless sounds and as the last sound of a phrase, it should not be completely unvoiced. Even at the end of a sentence, *his* should not sound like *hiss,* *fleas* like *fleece,* *pays* like *pace,* or *cards* like *carts.*

Because the / s / and / z / are so troublesome, we want to give some extra attention to their production. Here are some general principles to guide you:

1. Be certain that the tongue tip position is correct. These sounds may be articulated on either upper or lower gum ridge, but the tongue should not hang somewhere in between. Correct placement is absolutely essential if these sounds are not to be distorted.

2. Adequate tongue tension is also required for the correct production of the / s / and / z /. Push the tongue tip firmly against the ridge. A lax tongue will produce a distorted sound.

3. A third requisite for satisfactory production of these sounds is teeth occlusion. Your upper front teeth and your lower front teeth must be brought together, lightly touching or a little apart. Do not worry about the back teeth or the side teeth; check on the two center upper teeth and the two center lower ones. Even if you have a severe overbite—perhaps especially if you have a severe overbite—you must line up the front teeth. Remember that the lower jaw is perfectly capable of movement!

4. You must direct the breath stream over the top of the tongue tip and out of the front of the mouth. You can check to see if the air stream is being emitted in the center of the mouth by holding your index finger in front of the lips in the center of the mouth. Make an / s / sound. You should be able to feel the air stream hitting the finger. No air should come out of the sides of the mouth.

5. Finally, be sure that you emit an adequate amount of breath, but only an adequate amount of breath. Do not unduly prolong the sound.

Materials for Practicing / s /   and   / z /

Remembering to articulate the alveolar sounds with a firm tongue tip on the gum ridge and to give the / s / no more duration than you give to / t / and / d /, try the following sequences:

dick	tick	stick
dare	tare	stare
dough	toe	stow
dock	tock	stock
deem	team	steam
dill	till	still
Dan	tan	Stan
die	tie	sty
doubt	tout	stout
dub	tub	stub

Try these sequences, keeping the / s / tight against the gum ridge, focused forward, and brief:

stand	sand	snap	sap
steak	sake	snake	sake
steam	seem	sneak	seek
stage	sage	snail	sail
stag	sag	snag	sag
still	sill	snip	sip
stick	sick	snob	sob
stoop	soup	snooze	Sue's
stuck	suck	snort	sort
stir	sir	snoop	soup
stone	sown	snow	sew
stalk	Salk	sneeze	seize

slat	sat
slash	sash
slam	Sam
slater	satyr
slave	save
sled	said
sleep	seep
slick	sick
slew	sue
sleigh	say
slide	side
sling	sing
slub	sub
slur	sir
sly	sigh

Materials for Practicing / s /   and   / z / (continued)

rate	trait	straight
rap	trap	strap
ray	tray	stray
rip	trip	strip
rain	train	strain
rue	true	strew
ride	tried	stride
ripe	tripe	stripe
raid	trade	strayed
ruck	truck	struck
sap	passer	pass
same	Macy's	mace
sum	mussing	muss
sail	assail	lace
sign	nicer	nice
set	Tesser	Tess
sake	casing	case
sought	tossing	toss
zeal	pleasing	lees
zone	nosey	nose
zoom	amusing	moos
Zeus	Susan	sues

1. Stop, look, and listen!
2. It's all the same to me, of course.
3. But it isn't the same thing.
4. I've already said I was sorry.
5. We've chosen our silver pattern.
6. Spring is his favorite season.
7. I'm concerned about whether it is constitutional.
8. Many of us have strong feelings about civil liberties.
9. Ozzie is afraid of snakes.
10. Nobody seemed to understand the lecture, but everybody took copious notes.
11. I lost my gloves, but Eddie gave me his.
12. Who says that crime never pays?

13. Spring is sprung; the grass is rizz.
    I wonder how far Vassar is.—*Burma Shave.*
14. Star light, star bright;
    First star I've seen tonight.
15. He can certainly perform mysterious tricks with those cards.
16. The audience liked the last scene best of all.
17. It takes me all week to read the Sunday *New York Times.*
18. The assignment was to read all of *Tom Jones.*
19. He's a master of the art of telling little harmless lies.
20. If he's working on a Ph.D., he's dying by degrees.
21. She's having a hard time raising money for her fees this semester.

/ ʃ / and / ʒ /

If you purse the lips slightly, occlude the front upper and lower teeth, place the front of the tongue blade either near the hard palate or behind the lower gum ridge, press the sides of the tongue against the sides of the hard palate or against the inner surfaces of the side teeth, and shoot the air stream out of the grooved tongue over the front of the tongue blade and between the teeth, you will produce a lingua-palatal fricative. There are two such fricatives in English: one that is voiceless (the first consonant in the word *assure*), represented by / ʃ /; and one that is voiced (the first consonant in the word *azure*), represented by / ʒ /.

You will notice several differences between the production of these sounds and of / s / and / z /. First, the lips are usually spread for / s / and / z / and are pursed for / ʃ / and / ʒ /. Second, the air stream is shot out over the tongue tip on / s / and / z / but comes over the front of the tongue on / ʃ / and / ʒ /. Also, the groove of the tongue is wider on / ʃ / and / ʒ / than on / s / and / z /, and the entire tongue is pulled farther back on / ʃ / and / ʒ /.

There are three common distortions of the / ʃ / and / ʒ / sounds: (1) dentalization, (2) lateral emission of the air, and (3) unvoicing of the / ʒ /.

If you dentalize the / s / and / z /, it is likely that you will also make the / ʃ / and / ʒ / with the tongue touching the front teeth. Placing the front of the tongue on the teeth will distort these sounds; correct tongue placement is essential to production of acoustically satisfactory sounds.

As in the case of / s / and / z /, the air should come over the center of the tongue on the / ʃ / and / ʒ /. The air stream should not come out over the sides of the tongue. If you have a problem with lateral emission, refer to page 38.

If you tend to unvoice voiced consonants, you should check to be certain that you do not unvoice / ʒ /. *Vision* should not rhyme with *fission*, nor *mirage* with *Dear Osh*.

Materials for Practicing / ʃ / and / ʒ /

shown	luscious	flesh
shine	machine	wash
shoot	ashamed	blush
shake	conscience	leash
shout	issue	brandish
shy	caution	harsh
shame	anxious	gauche
shower	ocean	lush
shun	mission	wish
shock	passion	gnash
sugar	patient	blemish

azure	rouge
confusion	camouflage
casual	entourage
vision	mirage
occasion	corsage
pleasure	garage

1. She never seems to agree with my decisions.
2. Various pressure groups determined the outcome of the election.
3. I'm going to the garage to have the car washed.

4. Will you show us where the treasure is hidden?
5. Harsh punishments are usually reserved for felons.
6. Occasionally he comes with his entire entourage.
7. At the last session of the English Parliament, there was great confusion in the Commons.
8. The corsage complemented the gown, which was beige.
9. Such intrusions are usually rather embarrassing.
10. We offered to furnish the professor with a new set of illustrations.
11. The doctor cautioned me to use sugar substitutes.
12. We should be free from unreasonable search and seizure.
13. The dinner was delicious, as usual.
14. I assure you that I will not shirk my duties, since failure would damage my prestige.
15. Without twinge of conscience, they shrieked with pleasure.

/ h /

If you bring the vocal bands together enough to cause friction but not vibration and huff the air through, you will produce the glottal fricative, which we represent by / h /. This sound occurs in English only at the beginning of a syllable and is usually voiceless, although when it occurs in the middle of a word between vowels it is sometimes voiced. Compare your own pronunciation of the word *half* and *behalf*. In forming both allophones of / h / the lips and tongue are in the position of the vowel that follows. Pronounce the words *he, had,* and *who* and you will see that the articulators are already in position for the following vowel when the / h / is uttered.

There are two common problems associated with the / h / sound: (1) omission, and (2) overaspiration.

In some areas of the United States (especially in metropolitan New York) the / h / is omitted by most speakers in such words as *hue* and *human*. Even cultivated speakers will make homonyms of *hue* and *you* and of *human* and *Youman*. In most of this country, however, omission of the / h / in such words is considered substandard and should be avoided.

If too much air is pushed through on the / h / sound, your speech will sound breathy. Move off the / h / quickly and on to the next vowel; do not huff and puff too forcefully on the / h / sound.

Glides

The glides differ from the other consonants in two major regards: (1) the articulators move from one position to another in the formation of these sounds, and (2) there is less obstruction of the air stream on glide sounds than on most of the other consonants. In connection with the first difference, you should remember that glides always glide into a vowel. They never appear in final position in a syllable or before a consonant. Because of the second difference, glides are sometimes called semivowels. In fact, each of the glides moves from the position of one of the vowels and is, therefore, no more obstructed than its related vowel.

/ w /

If you put your lips and tongue in the position for the vowel in the word *boo,* let the vocal folds vibrate, and glide from this position into the next vowel, you will produce the voiced bilabial glide, which we represent by / w /. More specifically, the sound is formed by puckering the lips, letting the tongue tip rest behind the lower front teeth, raising the back of the tongue toward the soft palate, closing the velum, and vibrating the vocal folds. Although this sound is the voiced cognate of the / ʍ / sound, it lacks the fricative nature of its voiceless partner.

The only common distortion of the / w / sound is the substitution of / v / in the speech of some who have learned English as a second language and of those whose speech patterns have been influenced by those who learned English as a second language.

Materials for Practicing / w /

worse	verse
went	vent
wine	vine
wane	vain
Weiss	vice
wile	vile
wary	vary
we're	veer

1. Watch out! It's getting worse.
2. What does the weather vane on the church steeple symbolize?
3. Many humanitarians have been men of vast wealth.
4. Victory is its own reward.
5. It comes in various widths and a wide variety of lengths.
6. A wise voter will check on a candidate's views .

/ j /

If you put your tongue in the position for the vowel in the word *beet*, let your vocal folds vibrate, and glide from this position into the next vowel, you will produce the voiced linguapalatal glide, which we represent by / j /. The sound is made by letting the tongue tip rest behind the lower front teeth, raising the front of the tongue nearly to the hard palate, closing the velum, and vibrating the vocal folds. The lips are in position for whatever vowel follows.

Most native speakers of American English have no difficulty with the / j / in such words as *yes, yearning, yesterday, yellow,* and *unyielding*. In two other contexts, however, the / j / does offer some problems: (1) after / l /, (2) before / u / (the vowel in the word *boo*).

The spelling *lli* should be pronounced / lj / when it occurs in the middle of such words as *million, billion, stallion, hellion, billiards,* and such names as *Williams* and *Collier.* Of course, the / lj / also occurs in such phrases as *will you* and *tell you.* Careless speakers tend to omit the / l / in the / lj / combination.

Many people are confused about when to use the vowel / u / and when to precede that vowel with the glide / j /. Here are some general principles to guide you:

1. In initial position in the word, the spellings *u, eu,* and *ew* are pronounced / ju /.

2. Generally, after / p /, / b /, / k /, / m /, / f /, / v /, and / h /, the spellings *u, eu, ew, iew, and ue* are pronounced / ju /.

3. After / t /, / d /, and / n /, the spellings *u, eu, ue,* and *ew* are pronounced either / u /, / ju /, or / ɪu /. (See page 58 for a discussion of the vowel / ɪ /.) Although the use of / u / predominates nationally, the most careful speakers use either / ju / or / ɪu /. We would encourage you not to use the / u /, because it results in a number of unnecessary homonyms.

Materials for Practicing / ju /

The following words contain / u /:

to, too, two, do, noose

The following words contain / ju /:

uniform, unity, unify, union, eulogy, usury, uranium, usage

Words in the first column are pronounced with / u /; those in the second column are pronounced with / ju /:

coo	cue
poor	pure
do	dew
booty	beauty
who	hue
moo	mew
food	feud
voodoo	view do

Check your pronunciation in the following sentences of the sound you use after / t /, / d /, and / n /:

1. Tuesday there will be a meeting of the Tuna Packers Association.
2. Do you read the *Daily News?*
3. How many students were involved in the incident?
4. He wrote the words to the song, but he used an old tune.
5. The note will come due next week.
6. The police are on duty twenty-four hours a day.
7. It is impolite to call me stupid.
8. All of the duly elected officers have been impeached.
9. Mr. Newley has written a new play.
10. What can I possibly do with a bushel of tulip bulbs?

/ r /

Because the / r / sound is made by different people in different ways and in different regions in different ways, it is difficult to describe this consonant with exactness. In addition, because the / r / is a glide, which implies continuous movement of the tongue from the sound that precedes it to the sound that follows it, the surrounding sounds cause variation in the production of / r /.

If you put your tongue in the position for the vowel in the word *burr* (see pages 73–76 for a discussion of the vowels / ɝ / and / ɚ /), let the the vocal folds vibrate, and glide immediately into the vowel that follows, you will produce a lingua-alveolar glide, which we represent by / r /. More specifically, the sound is formed by pointing the tensed tip of the tongue upward to a position just back of the alveolar ridge or by slightly curling the raised tongue tip back toward the palate, closing the velum, and vibrating the vocal folds. From this position, the tongue slides toward the position of the vowel which follows. If the following vowel is made in the back of the mouth, more than likely the tongue tip will be slightly retroflexed on the / r /. If the vowel following is made in the front of the mouth, more than likely the tongue tip will be slightly turned toward the alveolar ridge. You should remember in forming this sound that there should be a minimum of lip movement. The sound is articulated chiefly by the movement of the tongue!

There are four common distortions associated with the / r / sound: (1) trilled or flapped / r /, (2) excessive friction, (3) excessive retraction, and (4) labialization.

In certain other English-speaking countries, the / r / is either trilled or flapped against the ridge or palate. In the United States, however, trilling or flapping the / r / is uncommon and is considered an affectation. We advise against it.

If you push the air stream with considerable force through the opening between the tongue tip and the palate when making the / r /, the sound will possess a fricative quality. In the speech of most Americans, fricative / r / is unusual except in the consonant combinations / tr / and / dr /. Even in those combinations you should be careful not to attack the / r / sound with too much force. The slight devoicing of the / r / which occurs after the voiceless sounds in the combinations / pr /, / tr /, / kr /, / fr /, / θr /, and / ʃr / seems to increase the danger of excessive friction. If you have discovered that you tend to overaspirate some consonants, check to be certain that you do not push too much air through on the / r /, especially in these combinations.

In many parts of the United States, especially in the Middle West, the / r / is often produced with the tongue tip turned backward toward the palate. If this retroflexion is excessive, the vowels that surround the / r / will be distorted. You may have read a story in which an author spelled *very* as "vurry" and *American* as "Amurrucan" to represent this kind of pronunciation. If you produce the / r / with the tongue tip curled back toward the palate, check to be certain that you do not pull the tongue back so far that the vowels are noticeably distorted. Some speakers use another form of retracted / r / that sounds a great deal like the retroflex we have just discussed. In this variation, the tongue tip remains low in the front of the mouth and the back of the tongue is raised toward the soft palate. This retraction of the tongue, like excessive retroflexion, markedly changes the quality of the adjacent vowels and should be avoided.

The labialized / r / results from excessive lip movement in forming the sound and produces a distorted consonant which sounds something like / w /. If you discovered that you tended to labialize the / l /, you may also discover that you substitute lip movement for tongue movement on the / r /. Pronounce the word *red* and listen to determine if it sounds like *wed*. Next, check with a mirror to see if you are moving your lips as you pronounce the / r /. When / r / is the initial sound in a word, the lips will be in the position for the sound that follows while the / r / is being uttered. In the word *reed*, then, the lips should be spread for the vowel in the word and should not move while the / r / is being emitted. Most people who have difficulty with the labialized deviation of / r / do not lift the tongue tip up to the alveolar ridge or the palate but instead let the tongue tip lie low in the front of the mouth and raise the back of the tongue up toward the soft palate (in the position for / u / and / w /). To correct this distortion, you must raise your tensed tongue tip toward the proper spot and prevent the lips from moving. (Tongue tension is essential!)

Materials for Practicing / r /

wage	rage	weep	reap
will	rill	waste	raced
weak	reek	woos	ruse
woe	row	wound	round
won	run	wipe	ripe
wag	rag	wink	rink
west	rest	Wac	rack
wife	rife	wail	rail
weal	real	wig	rig

rear	career	Rome	aroma
round	around	rise	arise
rate	berate	rage	enrage
root	uproot	rye	awry
wrecked	direct	rive	arrive
robe	disrobe	ravel	unravel
ride	deride	ranged	deranged

Materials for Practicing / r / (continued)

rig	brig	ride	pride
reefer	briefer	roof	proof
rite	bright	rinse	prince
red	bread	rune	prune
wrought	brought	raid	prayed
rave	brave	rye	pry
rue	brew	reach	preach
rim	brim	rest	pressed
rain	train	rill	drill
rim	trim	raw	draw
rip	trip	ream	dream
raid	trade	rug	drug
rue	true	rive	drive
rash	trash	rain	drain
Rio	trio	rear	drear
right	trite	round	drowned
reek	creek	round	frowned
ram	cram	rock	frock
rum	crumb	rend	friend
ruse	cruise	ride	fried
rave	crave	runt	front
ripped	crypt	wrench	French
ride	cried	rank	frank
rest	crest	rail	frail
raze	graze	rift	thrift
rid	grid	rob	throb
reeve	grieve	rush	thrush
ripe	gripe	roan	throne
rope	grope	rash	thrash
round	ground	wrong	throng
rub	grub	rue	through
Rand	grand	rive	thrive

Materials for Practicing / r / (continued)

rude	shrewd	ray	spray
rink	shrink	rout	sprout
rill	shrill	ring	spring
rub	shrub	rightly	sprightly

raid	strayed	reach	screech
wrangle	strangle	rub	scrub
Ruggles	struggles	ream	scream
rip	strip	rue	screw

1. He would rather be Right than President.
2. I have been reading *Pride and Prejudice*.
3. If I broke it, I'm very sorry.
4. The customer is always right.
5. The new director will present his first play on Friday.
6. He eats french fries three times a day.
7. She's absolutely treacherous. Beware of her.
8. They sent me a crate of Florida oranges.
9. We'll cross that bridge when we come to it.
10. The train leaves at three o'clock and will arrive around five.
11. Pronounce the words carefully but not pedantically.
12. The store is demanding proof of payment.
13. The company will try to make other arrangements for the irate passenger.
14. His demands were pretty unrealistic.
15. We had a grand time on our trick-or-treat expedition.
16. Straight-laced and prudish, she brands everything obscene.

Affricates. An affricate is, phonetically, a combination of two consonants—a plosive and a fricative—but it is, phonemically, a single sound. That is to say, an affricate functions in the language as a single unit, and speakers of English do not recognize an affricate as two separate and divisible sounds. The / ts / in the word *mates* and the / dz / in the word *maids* are combinations of a plosive and a fricative, but they are not affricates because each individual sound retains its own identity.

There are two affricates in English. One is a combination of voiceless consonants and is the first and last sound in the word *church;* the other is a combination of voiced consonants and is the first and last sound in the word *judge.*

If you put your tongue tip in the position to form a / t /, making a good firm stop, and release the air in a / ʃ /, you will produce a voiceless affricate that we represent by / tʃ /.

If you put your tongue in the position to form a / d /, making a good firm stop, and then release the air in a / z /, you will produce a voiced affricate that we represent by / dʒ /.

There are four common distortions associated with the affricates: (1) incomplete closure, (2) dentalization, (3) lateral emission of the air, and (4) unvoicing of the / dʒ /.

Failure to block the air stream on the affricates, as on the plosives, is a mark of careless, slovenly speech. The name *Fitchen* should not sound like *fission,* and *ledger* should not be pronounced like a variation of *leisure.*

The affricates should begin with the tongue tip firmly on the gum ridge. If you have found that you tend to dentalize the / t / and / d /, check to see if you also dentalize the / tʃ / and / dʒ /.

The affricates belong to the family of high-frequency hissing noises known as sibilants. If you have a problem of emitting the air over the sides of the tongue on the / s /, / z /, / ʃ /, and / ʒ /, it is likely that you will also have a problem with lateral emission of the air on the affricates. Like other voiced sounds, / dʒ / will be slightly devoiced before voiceless sounds and when final in a phrase, but the / dʒ / should not be completely unvoiced. *Ridge* should not become *rich, besiege* should not be pronounced *beseech,* and *edging* should not be turned into *etching.*

Materials for Practicing / tʃ / and / dʒ /

etching	edging
lunches	lunges
riches	ridges
batches	badges

Materials for Practicing / tʃ / / dʒ / (continued)

searching   surging
breeches   bridges
lecher   ledger
beseeches   besieges

cheap	jeep	chest	jest	march	Marge
chip	gyp	choose	Jews	match	Madge
chunk	junk	chill	Jill	etch	edge
char	jar	chock	jock	rich	ridge
choke	joke	chutes	Jutes	lunch	lunge
cheer	jeer	chin	gin	search	surge
chinks	jinx	chug	jug	batch	badge
chain	Jane	chump	jump	leech	liege

1. It's a question seldom asked, even in speech classes.
2. A change in address must be reported at once.
3. He left the judge, determined to seek his revenge.
4. He got it off his chest by confessing to Student Board.
5. The politicians were accused of gerrymandering.
6. The performer is quite agile. No one else has such grace.
7. He has a vivid imagination; he should be watched.
8. Two cars in every garage is no longer a joke.
9. He sends Madge casual messages. Would you deliver them?
10. I hate pigeons. You're not well-adjusted.
11. I'll meet you at the general's house.
12. "Righteous indignation" may be a cloak for malicious vengeance.
13. He was ordered to squelch the rumors about the stranger.
14. He placed just above the median. The coach is pleased.
15. Who's catching a cold? The doctor urged us to get flu injections.
16. The cheering section was slow to catch on. They jumped to conclusions.
17. Nature speaks to all men; the Church speaks to a few.
18. Discourtesy was a major factor in his failure.

19. The mob surged into the street. Urchins followed them.
20. He ripped his breeches in the second match.
21. The soldier has asked for a hardship discharge.
22. Omitting lunch saves time for study. Cheating is inexcusable.
23. Each jar of peanut butter was judged individually.
24. Who could have chosen a better arrangement?
25. Each citizen has a responsibility to the general welfare.

Vowels

We have already defined vowels as speech sounds that are
emitted with relatively little obstruction of the air stream. Vowels,
then, are not articulated in the same way as consonants but
are distinguished one from another by slight changes in resonance in the oral cavity. By shifting the tongue around in the
mouth and by changing the shape of the opening formed by
the lips we produce the different vowels of American English.
We cannot be nearly so exact in describing the formation of
vowels as of consonants, because we cannot be precise in describing the height to which the tongue is raised on any given sound
or the exact degree to which the lips are rounded, because vowels
are influenced by the consonants that follow and precede them
and because different people produce the same vowels differently.
We will have to discuss the production of each vowel in rather
general terms, and you will have to train your ears to recognize
the slight differences that will distinguish one vowel from another.

Vowels are not classified in the same ways as consonants, because all vowels are voiced sounds (produced by vibration of
the vocal folds) and because all English vowels are emitted in
the same manner—through the mouth. (In some other languages
which have nasal as well as oral vowels, manner of emission is an
element of classification.)

Although duration of the sounds (vowels differ in their characteristic length) and the tension of the oral cavity (vowels differ
in the amount of tension or laxness of the tongue in forming the
sounds) are relevant to a complete study of vowels, for our purpose we have classified the vowels in English only in terms of
(1) the position of the tongue, and (2) the position of the lips.

(1) Position of the Tongue. When you form all the vowels, your tongue tip remains behind your lower front teeth. It is the rest of the tongue that moves around in the mouth to produce the different vowels. If you raise the front of the tongue high in the mouth up near the hard palate and, while the vocal folds are vibrating, slowly lower the front of the tongue until the tongue lies flat in the mouth, you will produce a number of vowel sounds that are called front vowels. Similarly, if you round the lips tightly and raise the back of the tongue high up in the back of the mouth near the soft palate and, while the vocal folds are vibrating, slowly lower the tongue and gradually relax the rounding of the lips, you will produce a number of vowel sounds that are called back vowels. In addition to the front and back vowels, there is a group of vowels made with the middle of the tongue raised in the middle of the mouth that are called, logically enough, middle vowels.

Each vowel in each of the groups can be further described in terms of the relative height to which the highest part of the tongue is raised to make the sound. For example, the vowel in the word *be* is made with the front of the tongue raised very high in the mouth; it is, therefore, called a high front vowel. The vowel in the word *boo*, on the other hand, is made with the back of the tongue raised very high in the mouth; it is a high back vowel. (*See* Figures 2–4, 2–5, and 2–6.)

(2) Position of the Lips. If you look in a mirror at the position of your lips as you pronounce the vowels in the words *moo, me,* and *ma,* you will notice that the lips are tightly rounded for the first, unrounded and spread for the second, and unrounded and quite open for the third. Vowels may be classified as to whether or not they are uttered with the lips rounded. In general, the lips are more or less spread for the front vowels, and they are more or less rounded for the back vowels.

FRONT VOWELS
/ i /

If you lift the front of the tongue nearly to the hard palate while the tip of the tongue rests behind the lower front teeth,

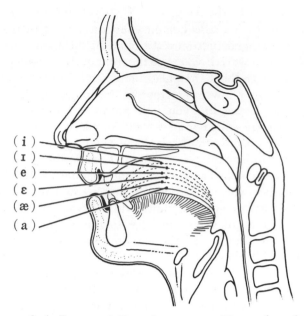

F I G U R E 2–4. Representative   tongue   positions   for   front
vowels. Reprinted with permission of The Macmillan Company
from Jon Eisenson, *The Improvement of Voice and Diction*, 2d
ed. Copyright © The Macmillan Company, 1965.

tense the tongue, spread the slightly tensed lips into a smile, and
emit the air stream through the mouth with the vocal folds vibrating, you will produce the highest front vowel, the vowel sound in
the word *beat* which we represented by / i /.

/ ɪ /

If you allow the front of the tongue to relax into a position
slightly lower and farther back than the height it assumed for
/ i /, relax the lips slightly but continue to leave them spread,
and emit the air stream through the mouth with the vocal folds
vibrating, you will produce the vowel in the word *bit,* which we
represent by / ɪ /. In addition to the higher elevation of the
tongue for / i /, there are certain other differences between the

two vowels. / i / is a tense vowel, whereas / ɪ / is more lax; / i /is usually long in duration, whereas / ɪ / is usually short.

There are two common distortions of this vowel: (1) substitution of / i / for / ɪ /, and (2) diphthongation.

In the middle of a word before a syllable beginning with a consonant, the spelling *i* is usually pronounced either / ɪ / or / ə / (the neutral first vowel in the word *above*). Speakers of standard American English do not use / i / in the middle of such words as *beautiful, pitiful, easily, medicine,* and *citizen.* Some speakers who have learned English as a second language substitute the / i / for the / ɪ / not only in the instances just cited but also in most words where the sound occurs. You have probably heard a foreign student say *eat* for *it, seat* for *sit,* and *team* for *Tim.* If you have this problem, produce the / i / sound, and while you are emitting the vowel, slightly relax the tongue and lips and lower the tongue a fraction in the mouth. The sound you produce will be the / ɪ /.

In the South and Southwest, there is a tendency on the part of some speakers to "drawl," which means that they elongate their vowels into diphthongs and triphthongs. / ɪ / is a short sound, and if it is unnecessarily prolonged it may become a diphthong / ɪə /. *It,* then, would become / ɪət / or even / ɪjət /. This lengthening and diphthongizing is substandard all over the country and is not characteristic of standard Southern and Southwestern speech.

Materials for Practicing / i /   and   / ɪ /

		each	itch		
		eat	it		
		e'en	in		
		eel	ill		
		ease	is		
leave	live	seal	sill	seep	sip
leak	lick	feel	fill	leap	lip
meal	mill	meat	mit	reach	rich
peal	pill	leafed	lift	cheat	chit
seems	Simms	heat	hit	peach	pitch

1. It is not easy to describe a beautiful woman.
2. I did not mean to imply that you were ignorant—just stupid.
3. There are clear indications that it will end in disaster.
4. I agreed with the teacher's interpretation, and still he flunked me.
5. I'll speak to him this evening.
6. Penniless and weary, he ended up on skid row.
7. I believe that he is the most creative person I know.
8. I resent a person with a holier-than-thou attitude.
9. We react emotionally rather than logically.
10. She is completely out of touch with reality.
11. He complained that the meat was full of gristle.
12. Eager to please, the minister rewrote the sermon.
13. Is he coming in his new automobile? No, he's still driving the old one.
14. Dick is the leader in the class that meets on Wednesday evening.
15. Some of our citizens are easily influenced by demagogues.

/ e /

If you open the lips a bit more and spread them a bit less than for producing / ɪ /, lift the front of the tongue to a position slightly below the height it assumed to produce / ɪ /, and emit the air stream through the mouth with the vocal folds vibrating, you will produce the first vowel in the word *chaotic,* which we represent by / e /. This sound occurs as a pure vowel only in unstressed syllables in American English and is heard much more commonly as the first vowel of the dipththong in the word *say,* which we represent by / eɪ /. The sound / e /, made with the tensed front of the tongue raised midway in the front of the mouth, is called a tense mid-front vowel.

Most Americans have no difficulty with this sound, but non-native speakers often substitute the pure vowel for the more common diphthong. This distortion occurs because the speaker is not adding the off-glide vowel of the diphthong. See page 77 for a more complete discussion of the diphthong / eɪ /.

/ ε /

If you open the lips just a bit more than you did for forming the / e /, allow the front of the tongue to relax into a position slightly lower and farther back than the height it assumed for / e /, and emit the air stream through the mouth with the vocal folds vibrating, you will produce the vowel in the word *bet*, which we represent by / ε /.

Both / e / and / ε / are mid-front vowels, but / ε / is more lax in its tongue tension than / e /, lower in tongue position than / e /, and usually shorter in duration than / e /.

There are four common distortions of the / ε /: (1) substitution of / eɪ /, and (2) substitution of / ɪ /, (3) substitution of / æ /, and (4) diphthongation.

Some speakers in the South distort this vowel by substituting the higher, tenser mid-front vowel for the lower, laxer one. Perhaps you have heard someone say *head* as *haid* and *leg* as *laig* to represent this sound deviation. Be certain to use the / ε / in such words as *leg, keg, egg, beg, bed, measure,* and *pleasure*.

A second distortion which, though substandard, is quite common in the South, Middle West, and Southwest is the substitution of / ɪ / for the / ε / before consonants made on the gum ridge. Anticipating the coming consonant, the speakers lift the tongue to the / ɪ / position and replace the / ε / vowel with the higher vowel sound. This distortion is most likely to occur before the nasal sounds. But *ten soldiers* are not *tin* soldiers; a *pen* is not a *pin;* and *men* should be distinguished from *Min.*

Another distortion which you may sometimes hear is the substitution of / æ / for / ε /. In this case, the speaker is dropping the tongue down and back from the position of the / ε / so that he might say *yass* for *yes* and *gas* for *guess.*

Like the / ɪ /, the vowel / ε / is a short sound. If you elongate the sound there is a danger of turning it into a diphthong. If you discovered that you have a tendency to diphthongize the / ɪ / into / ɪe /, you may also find that you diphthongize the / ε / into / εə /. Pronounce the word *met*. Do you hold onto the vowel and get a little *uh* sound (/ ʌ /) before the / t /? You then have substituted a diphthong for a pure vowel; you are drawling. Make the / ɛ / short, and move on to the following consonant quickly.

Materials for Practicing / ɛ /

edge	ledge
ebb	deb
end	lend
egg	leg
ember	member
ere	there
etch	wretch
Ed	bed

1. You can sing "Git Along, Little Doggies," but you should say "Get along!"
2. Women outnumber men in the United States.
3. Ed has moved into a penthouse. The rent is exorbitant.
4. Ten and ten and two are twenty-two.
5. Yes, there is an echo in the auditorium.
6. I meant every word I said.
7. Please make an extra effort to be ready on time.
8. I guess I will lend him a few dollars from my paycheck.
9. He told me he was the sinner on the football team; I think he meant that he was the center.
10. The speaker used no gestures until the end of his speech.

/ æ /   and its variant   / a /

If you raise the front of the tongue to a position slightly below and behind the height it assumed for producing the / ɛ /, open the lips without much tension, and emit the air stream through the mouth with the vocal folds vibrating, you will produce the low front vowel that occurs in the word *bat* and which we represent by / æ /.

The vowel / æ / has a variant form, or allophone, which is heard mostly in New England. This second vowel, which may be used interchangeably with the first, is a lower front vowel than / æ /. It is about halfway between the vowel sound in *at* and that in *alm* and is represented by / a /.

There are three common distortions of the / æ /: (1) raising, (2) nazalizing, and (3) diphthongizing.

Not long ago one of our students told us that nothing was inevitable but death and Texas. The pronunciation of *Texas* for *taxes* is an extreme example of raising the vowel, because the speaker actually substituted / ɛ / for the / æ /. Most speakers who distort the vowel by tensing and raising the tongue do not go that far. You can check in the mirror to see if you raise the tongue on this sound. Watch to see where the tongue is when you pronounce the / ɛ /; then watch to see if it drops considerably to form the / æ /. It should drop so that the tongue is almost flat in the mouth on the low front vowel.

Many speakers who raise and front the / æ / also nasalize the vowel, producing a particularly unpleasant sound. Be especially careful when the vowel precedes a nasal consonant. Listen to your own pronunciation of such words as *can, Sam,* and *bang* to see if you detect excessive nasalization of the vowel. Next, pronounce the word *cad,* being certain not to raise and nasalize the vowel, and then pronounce the word *can,* trying to get the same open, oral vowel you produced in *cad.* Try the same procedure with *sad* and *Sam* and with *bad* and *bang.*

If you tend to drawl, you probably elongate the vowel / æ /. Some speakers stretch the simple vowel not just into a diphthong but into a triphthong. Have you ever heard someone say / mæjən / for *man?* Probably the substitution of the diphthong / æə / for the pure vowel is more common, but it is no more acceptable. Remember to move on to the next consonant; do not try to hang on to the vowel.

Materials for Practicing / æ /

add	Ann	sad	Sam
cad	can	cat	cam
mad	man	mad	ma'am
had	hand	hat	ham
dad	Dan	dad	damn
fad	fan	lad	lamb
bad	ban	rat	ram
pad	pan	pad	Pam

1. They passed the bandstand late in the afternoon.
2. Sam had a very bad time at the party.
3. His problem is that he cannot analyze facts.
4. I am not particularly happy with either candidate.
5. His car was badly damaged in the accident.
6. I will catch the last bus back home.
7. A few inaccurate answers kept me from passing the course.
8. After the excursion there was sand on the blanket.
9. There will be a mass meeting of the faculty this afternoon.
10. There are several aspects of the case I do not understand.
11. Dad thinks my present income is adequate.
12. Mr. Thatcher became rather angry with me.
13. His hostile attitude and nefarious activities were only two factors which led to his dismissal.
14. We have had a very happy time in Paris.
15. Francis is handsome, but he is not practical.
16. I think Ann is in the laboratory.
17. Allen has a habit of playing pranks on people.
18. He is too passive to be a good actor.
19. Ask me no questions and I'll not have to lie.

BACK VOWELS
/ ɑ /   and its variant   / ɒ /

If you let the tongue lie low in the mouth, open the unrounded lips rather wide, and emit the air stream through the mouth with the vocal folds vibrating, you will produce the low back vowel in the words *alms* and *arm*, which we represent by / ɑ /. It is no accident that the physician asks you to say *ah* when he wants to look down your throat; when you produce the / ɑ / you open the mouth wider and drop the tongue lower than on any other vowel in English.

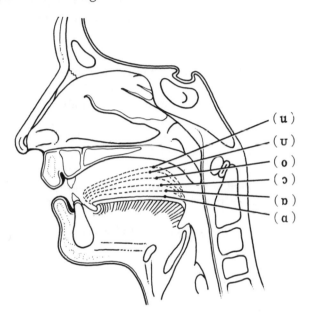

F I G U R E 2–5. Representative tongue positions for back vowels. Reprinted with permission of The Macmillan Company from Jon Eisenson, *The Improvement of Voice and Diction*, 2d ed. Copyright © The Macmillan Company, 1965.

The vowel / ɑ / has a variant form that is used by some speakers in place of the / ɑ / in "short *o*" words such as *odd, hot, pot,* and *stop*. This second vowel is a higher back vowel than the first. It is formed with the tongue slightly raised in back from the position of / ɑ / and with the lips slightly less open and more rounded than in the production of / ɑ /. This variant is ordinarily short and lax. (The vowel sound / ɒ / is substituted by some people in some words where most of us use the / ɔ /, the vowel in the words *all* and *ought*.)

The most common distortion of the / ɑ / is that of raising and fronting the vowel by pulling the tongue up and forward toward the position of / a / or /æ /. If the sound is made with undue tension with the tongue slightly lifted toward the front of the mouth and the lips slightly spread, the sound will be distorted. The / ɑ / should be open, free, and relaxed. Drop the tongue and open the mouth to form it.

Materials for Practicing / ɑ /

odd	ah	hah
ox	alms	palms
occupy	art	dart
otter	ark	park
obvious	arch	march
oblong	arm	harm
opposite	arbor	harbor

1. He was not qualified for a career in the army.
2. My partner will buy up the option.
3. Popeye and Olive were always in trouble.
4. No, my father was not a locksmith.
5. The guard was unable to prevent the robbery.
6. The golfer responded with an oath.
7. Obligations should be met without argument.
8. I don't object to giving alms, but I wouldn't give him a farthing!

/ ɔ /   and its variant   / ɒ /

If you raise the back of the tongue up slightly toward the soft palate, round the lips a bit more than you did in forming / ɑ /, and emit the air stream through the mouth with the vocal folds vibrating, you will produce the low back vowel in the words *all* and *ought,* which we represent by / ɔ /. To form this sound correctly, you must achieve slight tension of the tongue and lips, rounding the lips into a vertical ellipse.

As we noted earlier, the / ɒ / is used as an allophone, or variant form, of this vowel in some regions. An author trying to represent these dialectal differences with regular spelling might spell the word *forest* as *fawrest* or *fahrest* to indicate the difference in pronunciation. Check your own pronunciation of such words as *forest, dog, hog, log, Laura, Pauline,* and *called* to see which of the vowels you use in these words. Either is acceptable, but most speakers of American English use the / ɔ /, and in many parts of the country the / ɒ / would be thought an affectation.

There are two common distortions of the vowel / ɔ /: (1) retraction, and (2) diphthongizing. Indeed, they often occur together.

The distortion which we label "retraction" of the / ɔ / is produced by doing two things: first, by puckering the lips excessively so that they are noticeably protruded, and second, by pulling the tongue back in the mouth. You may have heard someone imitating the stereotyped impression of "New Yorkese" by asking for *cawfee* and for a *chawklet mawlted* or complaining that something was *awwful.* The retracted / ɔ / is a tense, grating sound and should be avoided. If you tend to retract the vowel, you should relax the lips slightly and open the mouth a bit wider, being certain that the lips are not protruded and do not move, and you should lift the back of the tongue to a position about halfway between / ɑ / and / o /.

Another deviation results from replacing the pure vowel / ɔ / with a diphthong. If you add the / ə /, the first vowel in the word *above,* to the / ɔ /, you have the diphthong / ɔə /. This elongation, common in the greater New York area, might be called a "Northern drawl"! Combined with retraction of the / ɔ /, it is a particularly unpleasant distortion to most American ears. In such words as *ought, taught, call, tall, talk, dog, coffee, awful, chocolate,* and *malted,* do not hold on to the / ɔ /; move on to the next consonant.

Materials for Practicing / ɔ /

all	tall	taw
oft	soft	saw
Ong	wrong	raw
awes	claws	claw
ought	naught	gnaw
off	cough	caw
orgy	Georgie	jaw
awed	laud	law

1. It was an ordeal, but I taught the class.
2. The wrestler lost points for stalling.
3. All of the pledges suffered horribly.
4. The author was quite proud of his lyrics for the song.
5. Most coffins cost a fortune!
6. Paul is going to Europe in August.
7. Please call a taxi for me about eight in the morning.
8. I'm sorry that we are losing our foreign trade.
9. We're learning to talk in flawless English.
10. I drank orange juice, coffee, and a chocolate malted for breakfast.
11. Because of recent reforms, it is easier to adopt an orphan.
12. I ought to buy that dog from my lawyer.

/ o /

If you raise the back of the tongue up about midway in the back of the mouth toward the soft palate, round the lips more than you did to form / ɔ /, and emit the air stream through the mouth with the vocal folds vibrating, you will produce the mid-back vowel we represent by / o /. This sound is heard in American English as a pure vowel in such unstressed syllables as the first syllables of *obey* and *hotel* and as the first vowel of the diphthong in such words as *know, grow,* and *blow.*

In unstressed syllables, the pure vowel is rarely distorted. Distortions of the diphthong / oʊ / will be discussed on page 84. The only common distortion of the / o / is the substitution of / ə / or / ɚ / when the vowel occurs at the end of a word. Such words as *potato, tomato, fellow, yellow, window, follow,* and *piano* should be pronounced with / o /. *Potato,* then, would not be either "puhtatuh" or "puhtater."

/ ʊ /

If you lift the back of the tongue up in back toward the soft palate farther than you did in forming the / o /, round the lips even more than you did on the / o /, and emit the air stream through the mouth with the vocal folds vibrating, you will produce the lax high back vowel heard in the word *look,* which we represent by / ʊ /. This vowel has much the same relation to the vowel sound in the word *Luke* (/ u /) as / ɪ / has to / i /. Just as / ɪ / is formed with the tongue slightly lower and more lax than on / i /, so / ʊ / is made with the tongue slightly lower and less tense than on / u /. Also, / i / and / u / are usually long sounds, and / ɪ / and / ʊ / are usually short in duration.

There are three common distortions of the / ʊ /: (1) medializing, (2) diphthongizing, and (3) substitution of / u /.

Some speakers make this vowel with the tongue too low and too far forward. Usually, speakers who medialize the / ʊ / not only raise the tongue in the middle of the mouth rather than in the back but also relax the lips somewhat. Carried to an extreme, medializing may result in the actual substitution of the middle vowel / ʌ / (heard in the words *mud* and *hut*) for the / ʊ /. *Look* should not sound like *luck,* *took* like *tuck,* or *shook* like *shuck.*

Like the other vowels, / ʊ / can be stretched into a diphthong. Be careful not to drawl this vowel. Move on to the next consonant, and keep the vowel pure.

Many foreign students substitute the / u / for the / ʊ / with the result that *could* sounds like *cooed,* *would* sounds like *wooed, pull* sounds like *pool,* and *full* resembles *fool.* If you have difficulty with this / ʊ /–/ u / confusion, you will have to train your ear to hear the difference and train your tongue and lips to relax slightly from the position of / u / to form the lower, laxer vowel / ʊ /.

/ u /

If you raise the back of the tongue nearly to the soft palate, round the lips tightly, and emit the air stream through the mouth with the vocal folds vibrating, you will produce the highest back vowel, heard in the words *Luke* and *Sue,* which we represent by / u /. / u / is usually a long vowel, and it is produced with the lips and back of the tongue tense.

There are three common distortions of the / u /: (1) substitution of / ʊ /, (2) medializing, and (3) diphthongizing.

If you fail to purse the lips tightly enough and to secure adequate tension of the tongue, you may lower the vowel / u / to the position of the lax high back vowel / ʊ /. This distortion should be avoided. Although the use of / ʊ / in such words as *root, roof, room, hoof,* and *hoop* seems to be increasing, we would encourage you to use the more commonly used / u /.

Some speakers distort the / u / by attempting to make it with the tongue too far forward in the mouth and the lips too relaxed. This medializing, or raising of the tongue in the middle of the mouth rather than at the back, distorts and "flattens" the sound. Work for adequate lip rounding and correct tongue placement.

As we said earlier, / u / is a long sound. Unless you are careful it can easily be turned into a diphthong. If you start with the tongue in a position too low to produce a good / u / and slide up to the right spot, you will, of course, produce a diphthong. Substitution of a diphthong for a pure vowel may also result from starting in the correct tense high position and relaxing into a lower spot. To avoid drawling, move definitely to the right place to form the sound, and hold the tongue in that place until you move on to the next sound.

Materials for Practicing / u / and / ʊ /

/ ʊ /	/ u /
full	fool
cookie	kooky
look	Luke
pull	pool
should	shooed
hood	who'd
wood	wooed

/ u /

ooze	choose	chew
oolong	too long	too
umiak	loom	lieu
oomph	zoom	zoo

1. I understood every word of the bulletin.
2. He may be foolish, but he is not crooked.
3. Both of them grew up in Brooklyn.
4. Who's going to help you review for the exam?
5. I would appreciate it if you could return my book.
6. You will rue the day you became a truant.
7. Mr. Cruse takes a little coffee in his sugar.
8. From soup to pudding the meal was delicious.
9. We put the Girl Scout cookies in a bushel basket.
10. A few truthful rumors can ruin a good neighborhood.

MIDDLE VOWELS
/ ʌ /

If you lift the middle of the tongue slightly toward the palate, keep the lips unrounded, and emit the air stream through the mouth with the vocal folds vibrating, you will produce the stressed middle vowel in the words *up* and *come,* which we represent by / ʌ /. It is ordinarily a short sound.

The most common distortion of the / ʌ / is fronting and raising the sound before consonants made in the front of the mouth. Pulling the tongue up and forward on the / ʌ / vowel results in its sounding much like / ɪ / or / ɛ /. *Just,* then, would be mispronounced *gist* or *jest.* Check your own pronunciation of such words as *such, cover, judge, hush, shut,* and *brush* to be certain that you do not substitute / ɪ / or / ɛ / for the / ʌ /.

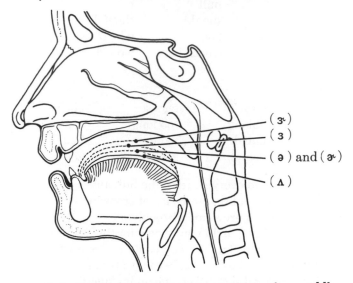

F I G U R E 2–6. Representative tongue positions for middle vowels. Reprinted with permission of the Macmillan Company from Jon Eisenson, *The Improvement of Voice and Diction,* 2d ed. Copyright © The Macmillan Company, 1965.

Materials for Practicing / ʌ /

1. Just a moment, please. You will get your money.
2. The judge was a bit rough on the defense attorney.
3. His coat was covered with mud.
4. Don't mumble when giving instructions to the class.
5. My uncle said that once was quite enough.
6. I'm hungry because I didn't have supper.

7. No one has a satisfactory definition for the word *love*.
8. Our club won the first contest.
9. After lunging at us, he stumbled and fell.
10. My brother likes his meat well done.
11. Come up to see us sometime.

/ ə /

The unstressed equivalent of / ʌ / is the short neutral middle vowel heard in the first syllable of the word *above*, which we represent by / ə /. This vowel is a lax vowel, made with the lips unrounded and the tongue raised slightly in the middle of the mouth. The most frequently used vowel in the language, it is called *schwa* and is used in most unstressed syllables. (Almost all vowels are reduced to this neutral vowel when they occur in unstressed syllables. Only the highest front vowel / i /, which often is weakened to / ɪ /, and the highest back vowel / u /, which often is weakened to / ʊ /, are exceptions.) The schwa commonly occurs in the unstressed forms of form words. (See page 105.)

/ ɝ /   and its variant   / ɜ /

If you lift your tongue tip upward to a position just back of the alveolar ridge, curl the raised tongue tip back slightly toward the hard palate, lift the middle of the tongue up near the hard palate, leave the lips unrounded, and emit the air stream through the mouth with the vocal folds vibrating, you will produce the stressed high-middle vowel heard in the words *sir* and *curr*, which we represent by / ɝ /. This stressed vowel is tense and long. The amount of retroflexion (which gives the sound its "*r* coloring") varies greatly from person to person and region to region.

There is a variant form, or allophone, of this vowel heard mostly in New England and New York City, which we represent by / ɜ /. If you arch the middle of the tongue toward the middle of the mouth as you would on / ɝ / but let your tongue tip lie low in the front of the mouth rather than curling it back behind the gum ridge, you will produce this variant which many Easterners and Southerners use in place of / ɝ /. The use of this *r*-less vowel seems to be decreasing even in New York City.

The only common distortion of the / ɝ / is excessive retraction. If you pull the tongue tip back too far toward the palate or the middle of the tongue back too far in the mouth, you will distort the vowel. This distortion is more common in the Middle West and Southwest than in the rest of the country.

Materials for Practicing / ɝ / or / ɜ /

err	dirty	myrrh
ermine	purple	burr
early	burly	cur
earn	servant	her
erstwhile	nervous	fur
Erwin	mercy	sir

1. The early bird can have the worm.
2. The quarterback turned before hurling the spheroid across the field.
3. For the third time, I refer you to your textbook.
4. I urge you to come to the rehearsal this evening.
5. They were deterred by their fear of violence.
6. She not only spurned his advances; she gave him a sermon.
7. The meeting adjourned without determining what to do next.
8. The driver averted a tragedy by swerving sharply to the right.
9. We are certain that you are informed and concerned about public affairs.
10. He never shirks a burden, and he serves without pay.
11. She may be earnest, but she erred.
12. Urchins followed us everywhere in the urban areas.

/ ɚ /

The unstressed equivalent of the stressed vowel / ɝ / is the short neutral vowel with an *r*-coloring heard in unaccented syllables that we represent by / ɚ /. You will see that the symbol is a schwa with a little *r* hook on it. Like the schwa it is used in unstressed syllables, and like the / ɝ / it is *r*-colored. It is more lax and shorter than the / ɝ /, made with the lips unrounded and the middle of the tongue raised toward the center of the mouth and the tip of the tongue curled back toward the palate behind the gum ridge. The air is emitted through the mouth with the vocal folds vibrating. As in the case of the stressed / ɝ /, the amount of retroflexion of the tongue tip varies greatly.

Most American speakers use the / ɚ / vowel when the letter *r* precedes a consonant. The sound would occur, then, before the final consonant in such words as *harm, heart, tired,* and *bored.* It also occurs in final position after vowels and diphthongs in such words as *ear, air, are, our,* and *ire.*

Speakers who use the / ɜ / rather than the / ɝ / also ordinarily use the / ə / in place of / ɚ /. These speakers would pronounce the word *mother* / mʌðə /, but if the next word in the phrase began with a vowel, they would put the *r* back in. *Mother and father,* then would be [mʌðərənfɑðə]. These speakers would also omit the "*r*-coloring" in such words as *card* (which they would simply pronounce with a lengthened / ɑ /) and *hour* (in which they would employ schwa in place of / ɚ /).

There are two common distortions of the / ɚ /: (1) excessive retraction, and (2) substitution of / ɔɚ /.

If you pull the tongue too far back toward the back of the mouth and curl the tongue tip too far back toward the palate, you will distort the sound. This vowel is a neutral, middle vowel —not a back vowel.

Some people who think in terms of pronouncing written letters rather than vocal sounds are led into "spelling mispronunciations." You may have heard someone say *educatawr* (/ ɛdʒukertɔɚ /) for *educator* (/ ɛdʒukertɚ / or *actawr* (/ æktɔɚ /) for *actor* (/ æktɚ /). This substitution results from a misunderstanding of the way language works and is pedantic, affected, and incorrect. The / ɚ / can be spelled many different ways: *er, or, ar, ir, ur, ure, yr, oar,* or *re*. Note your pronunciation of the following words: *other, educator, wizard, nadir, murmur, measure, satyr, cupboard,* and *theatre*. You should find that the same vowel (/ ɚ /) occurs in the last syllable of all the words.

Materials for Practicing / ɚ /

perform		surmount
perfume		survey (v.)
persuade		surmise
perhaps		survival

mother	humor	pleasure	scepter
father	actor	treasure	theater
bother	factor	pressure	pillar
brother	mirror	measure	tapir
murmur	murder	further	surfer

1. We cannot permit you to perjure yourself.
2. You must maintain your humor to survive.
3. I would rather not search for the treasure.
4. Weather hindered the surfers from practicing yesterday.
5. We persuaded him to walk under a ladder and break the mirror.
6. The performance will be given either this week or next.
7. My brother made his sacrifice at the altar.
8. Perhaps she can't be bothered with answering the phone.
9. It is no pleasure for an actor to memorize his lines.
10. The underprivileged have difficulty in surmounting their background.

Diphthongs. Diphthongs, like affricates, phonetically are blends of two sounds but phonemically are single units, because they strike the native listener's ear as a single sound. An affricate, you will remember, combines two consonants into a single sound unit; a diphthong combines two vowels, which listeners do not recognize as separate and divisible sounds, into a single sound unit.

There are five such diphthongs in American English. Beginning with a long, strong vowel and moving to a shorter, weaker vowel, three end in / ɪ / and two end in / ʊ /. The sentence "They buy no toys now" contains all five diphthongs.

/ eɪ /

As we observed earlier (page 60) the "long *a*" in English is ordinarily a diphthong rather than a pure vowel. Only in unstressed syllables, such as the first syllable of the word *chaotic,* does the pure vowel / e / occur. If you pronounce the word *bay* in slow motion, you will be able to tell that the front of your tongue moves on the "*a* sound" from the position of the / e / upward toward the position of / i /. It actually does not reach the / i / position and ends about / ɪ /. In any stressed syllable, native speakers of English will use this diphthong for the "long *a.*"

There are two distortions of the / eɪ /: (1) substitution of the pure vowel for the diphthong, and (2) substitution of / ɛ / or / æ /.

Native speakers of English do not confuse the / e / and / eɪ /, but some people who learned English as a foreign language may substitute a pure / e / for the diphthong. They may also make the vowel with a bit more tension of the tongue than native speakers. If you have this problem, you should train your ear to hear the distinction between the vowel and the diphthong and work to elongate the sound, moving from the tongue position of the first vowel to the second in one continuous movement.

Some speakers, particularly in the East, substitute either a distorted / ɛ / or / æ / for the / eɪ /, especially before / l /. Although some writers might not call this practice substandard, it is clearly uncommon and results in a number of homonyms. We would encourage you not to make this substitution. Check your own pronunciation of *Yale* and *yell* and *pail* and *pal.* Do you make a clear distinction between the two words in each pair?

Materials for Practicing / eɪ /

Differentiate between the vowel / ɛ / and the diphthong / eɪ /:

yell	Yale
bell	bale
sell	sale
well	wail
tell	tale
Vel	vale
dell	dale
fell	fail
hell	hail
jell	jail
Nell	nail
pell-mell	pale male

Try to keep the diphthong consistent in the following words:

Kaye	Kate	kale
pay	pate	pale
hay	hate	hale
Faye	fate	fail
way	wait	wail
tray	trait	trail
bay	bait	bail
stay	state	stale
day	date	dale
gray	great	grail
fray	freight	frail

1. Hail, fellow, well met.
2. Bill Bailey, won't you please come home?
3. We were sailing along on Moonlight Bay.
4. Is life a tale told by an idiot?
5. The motion failed for lack of a second.
6. Sally knows the jailer very well.
7. The mailman was late this morning.
8. Tony Zale was a famous pugilist.

9. Yale is in New Haven. Mail your entries there.
10. There seems to be no malice in Gail's attitude.
11. I have never seen Haley's Bar, but I have heard the ballyhoo.
12. Don't tell me the material is stale. Make up your own examples.

/ aɪ /

If you put your tongue in the position for producing either the vowel / a / or the vowel / ɑ / and then move smoothly into the position for / ɪ /, you will produce the diphthong heard in the word *buy*, which we represent by / aɪ / or / ɑɪ /.

There are two common distortions of this diphthong: (1) substitution of / a /, / aə /, / ɑ /, or / ɑə /, and (2) retraction.

You may have read stories in which the author spelled the word *I'm* as *Ah'm* in dialogue to represent the substitution of the vowel / ɑ / or the combination of the vowel / ɑ / plus the off-glide vowel / ə / for the diphthong / aɪ /. This distortion is not uncommon in the South and is characteristic of the speech of the less educated, although you may hear some educated speakers use it as well. Instead of the / ɑ /, some speakers substitute the lowest front vowel / a / or that vowel plus the off-glide / ə /. This "flattened sound" is also heard in the South, particularly in the mountain regions. We have heard huge cheering crowds in sports arenas urging their teams to [faət, faət, faət]! Actually, you will note, these speakers are having trouble with the second vowel of the diphthong. Either they omit the second vowel altogether and leave only the first pure vowel to substitute for the diphthong, or they substitute the schwa for the second vowel / ɪ /. Check your own pronunciation of the personal pronoun *I* to be certain that when the tongue moves from the / a / or / ɑ / the front of your tongue moves up to the position of / ɪ / in the front of your mouth rather than to the position of / ə / in the middle of your mouth. Use a mirror to check on the tongue movement.

In the metropolitan New York area, many speakers pull the tongue back to the back of the mouth on the opening vowel of the diphthong, and this retraction markedly distorts the sound. A few speakers actually substitute the / ɔ / for the / a / when they initiate this diphthong, so that the word *buy* sounds like *boy*. Most who retract the sound, however, instead substitute the / ɒ / for the first vowel of the diphthong. You must be certain that you do not round the lips on this sound and do not pull the tongue back as you begin the diphthong. The words *add* (or *odd*) and *I'd* should both start with the tongue and lips in about the same position.

Materials for Practicing / aɪ /

ice	lice	lie
ides	sides	sigh
I'll	Nile	nigh
I'm	time	tie
Ike	pike	pie
ire	fire	fie
I've	rive	rye
eyes	buys	buy

1. I have been invited to a student riot this weekend.
2. I had no idea you would try to bribe me!
3. I plan to buy an excellent item for my collection.
4. Perhaps you can get an idea of the size of the island from this diagram.
5. Time and tide are a temptation for surfers.
6. Sy is an aspiring politician.
7. The high jumper is trying for a record height.
8. Why are you buying a hundred pounds of ice?
9. Forgive me for prying, but what are your designs?
10. We can drive it in about five hours.
11. I will not sign the contract until I've read it.
12. We defied the ban and held the biennial meeting.
13. I was reminded that I have a prior commitment.
14. The rhyme scheme defies analysis!
15. Riding up the Nile was the most exciting experience of my life.

/ ɔɪ /

If you put your lips and tongue in the position for producing / ɔ / and move smoothly into the position for / ɪ /, you will produce the diphthong heard in the word *boy*, which we represent by / ɔɪ /.

There are three distortions associated with this diphthong: (1) substitution of / ɝ /, (2) substitution of / ɔə /, and substitution of / aɪ /.

Occasionally in metropolitan New York or in the South you may hear someone say *Berle* for *boil*, *earl* for *oil*, or *furl* for *foil*. It is considered substandard, and you should avoid it.

In the South you may also hear the substitution of / ɔə / for / ɔɪ /. As in the case of the diphthong / aɪ /, the problem arises on the off-glide portion of the diphthong; a schwa is substituted for the high front vowel / ɪ /. The result is that the word *oil* will sound like a drawled version of *all*, and *boil* will resemble *ball*. Be certain that the front of your tongue moves to the high front / ɪ / position at the end of the diphthong rather than to the center of the mouth.

One other distortion of the / ɔɪ / is heard from time to time in the South. You may hear a few speakers still say *bile* for *boil*, *tile* for *toil*, and *pint* for *point*. Like the other distortions we have discussed, this substitution is substandard and you should not use it.

Materials for Practicing / ɔɪ /

oil	boil	boy
ointment	appointment	poi
	joint	joy
	soil	soy
	coin	coy
	Reuters	Roy
	toil	toy

1. The boys were forced to eat oysters during the initiation.
2. The royal family seemed to enjoy the performance.
3. He was anointed with oil and water.

4. The most poignant moment of the play was ruined by a noise in the audience.
5. Why would anyone want to join an organization in such turmoil?
6. Joyce tried to avoid my glances.
7. Reuters and Tass were embroiled in a controversy over the story.
8. She thought the poi had poisoned her.
9. The noise seemed to be coming from an adjoining room.
10. Roy has unusual poise on the speaking platform.
11. Ointment was applied to the wounds quickly.
12. Mr. Boyd collects old coins.

/ aʊ /

If you start with your lips and tongue in position for forming the / a / and glide from that vowel smoothly into the / ʊ /, you will produce the diphthong heard in the words *bough* and *now*, which we represent by / aʊ /. You can also start from the position of / ɑ / in the same way that you can begin the *i* diphthong with / ɑ /. / aʊ / is the more common of the two variants, but both are standard.

There are three common distortions of this diphthong: (1) fronting and raising, (2) nasalization, and (3) substitution of either / a / or / æ /. Of all the diphthongs, this one is the most frequently distorted in all sections of the United States; and of all the diphthongs, this one, when distorted, is the most unpleasant.

If you begin the diphthong with the tongue raised too high in the front of the mouth, you will produce a flat and very unpleasant sound. If you tend to raise the / æ / vowel, you should be especially careful in producing this diphthong. You may find that you not only substitute / æʊ / for / aʊ / but that you substitute a diphthong initiated with a raised form of / æ /. The / aʊ / should begin with the mouth open and the tongue relatively flat in the mouth. If you are not certain that you are producing the sound correctly, check with a mirror.

Many speakers who raise and front the diphthong also nasalize it. The result is that the sound is not only "flattened" but it is also "pinched" through the nose. This nasalized form is more likely to occur before the nasal consonants, but it can occur when it is neither preceded nor followed by an / m /, / n /, or / ŋ /. You must work to be sure that the velum fully closes off the passage to the nose, that the mouth is open, and that the air stream is emitted only through the mouth. Pronounce the word *how*. Now hold your nose and pronounce the word again. It should sound exactly the same, and you should not feel any air trying to come out of the nose while you say the word. If there is air trying to come out of the nose, then you are nasalizing the sound and you need practice to make the diphthong oral rather than nasal.

In the South, some careless speakers may shorten the diphthong by omitting the second vowel. / aʊ / then becomes just / a / or perhaps / æ /. Needless to say, this substitution of / a / or / æ / for the diphthong is substandard.

Materials for Practicing / aʊ /

owl	howl	how
out	rout	row
ounce	bounce	bough
hour	sour	sow

1. He was astounded that we couldn't tell a noun from a verb.
2. The college does not allow its students to carouse during school hours.
3. How can the college increase its endowment?
4. She seemed very proud of her new gown.
5. I doubt that I'll be able to meet you at the lounge.
6. The announcer took a bow with the rest of the cast.
7. The coach frowned when the center missed the rebound.
8. The queen was crowned at the witching hour.
9. When she gets angry, she goes in the house and pouts.

10. Outline the entire chapter, and count all the arguments.
11. The car was impounded by the town constable.
12. The weatherman has predicted showers, but you can't count on what he says.
13. What are the grounds for divorce in this state?
14. He was standing on the tower shouting like a madman.
15. Why are you out prowling now?

/ oʊ /

If you round the lips and raise the tongue a little over halfway up in the back of the mouth (to form the / o /) and then glide into the sound / ʊ / by rounding the lips further and raising the back of the tongue higher, you will produce the diphthong heard in the words *beau, so,* and *blow,* which we represent by / oʊ /. We discussed the pure vowel / o / on page 68, and noted there that the pure vowel is heard in American English only in unstressed syllables. In all instances where the "long *o*" occurs in stressed syllables, American speakers will use the diphthong / oʊ /.

There are only two deviations associated with this diphthong: (1) substitution of / o /, and (2) medializing.

Non-native speakers of English sometimes substitute the pure vowel / o / for the diphthong / oʊ /. If you fail to add the second vowel, the off-glide, pronounce the diphthong in slow motion and watch your lips and tongue movement in the mirror. You should see the lip opening close down considerably during the production of the sound, and you should be able to feel the tongue pull up in back as it moves from the / o / position to the / ʊ /.

Some speakers pull the entire diphthong forward by lifting the tongue in the center of the mouth rather than in the back. This medializing of the sound results in a distortion that causes *home* to sound something like *hum, most* like *must,* and *soak* like *suck.* In our judgment, this substitution of / ʌ / for / oʊ / is substandard and should be avoided.

Materials for Practicing / oʊ /

oh	float	flow
owed	rowed	roe
oaf	loaf	low
oak	soak	sew
own	blown	blow
oar	door	dough
oat	tote	toe

1. He took part in all the sports available at the resort.
2. I do not believe he will grow any more.
3. The owner could not agree that the cloth should be torn.
4. The speaker did not know how bored the audience really was.
5. Open the door slowly.
6. The crowd roared the chants they had learned by rote.
7. Fort Knox is where the gold is stored.
8. Is it only the cheerleaders who are hoarse all the time?
9. She insisted that I row toward the shore.
10. I'm told you're an expert on Indian folklore.

Sounds in Combination

Thus far we have discussed only individual sounds. But sounds do not occur in isolation; nobody talks a sound at a time. And sounds put together in groups are different from the sounds uttered alone. Let us, then, turn our attention to a few of the common groups of sounds that offer difficulties for many speakers of American English.

Consonant Combinations

TWO DIFFERENT PLOSIVES. You will remember that we defined stop-plosives as sounds on which the air stream was stopped completely by the articulators and the built-up air pressure was released in a little explosion. We also noted that the stop-plosives always stop the air, but they do not always explode. When the plosives come together one after another, there is only one explosion, although there are two stops. You stop the first consonant with a good firm closure but do not release it in a plosion; then you stop the second plosive with a complete closure and release it in a plosion. Check what you do when you say the word *act*, for example. The / k / closes off the air stream for an instant, but you do not explode the / k / as you would in the word *keep*. Instead, you move on to the closure for the / t / and explode only the second plosive. The same thing occurs even if the two plosives are in different words. Note that the / t / is stopped but not exploded and the / d / both stopped and exploded in the words *hot dog*. Check in such words as *back door, hot drink, hop down, sad case, big caldron,* or *rib cage* to be certain that you fully obstruct the air stream for an instant on the first stop-plosive and that you voice it if it should have vocal vibration.

Materials for Practicing Consecutive Plosives

1. He was in a ba*d p*osition.
2. He began to dro*p b*ehind rather quickly.
3. They mus*t b*egin at once.
4. Tom carried the pac*k d*ownstairs.
5. They said it couldn'*t b*e done.
6. The performance was qui*te g*ood.
7. Ho*p d*own from the bar, toad.
8. Be sure to pic*k g*ood examples.
9. Pupils are not allowe*d t*o do homework.
10. It's a waste*d t*wo points.
11. It was har*d t*o get him to do that.
12. I can'*t b*elieve that they have turne*d t*o alcohol!
13. They ma*de t*wo touchdowns in the las*t q*uarter of the game.
14. Don'*t b*e satisfied with slack articulation of the plosives.
15. He lived in the high ren*t d*istrict.
16. The hi*p b*one's connecte*d t*o the thigh bone.
17. Grea*t d*ay in the morning!
18. I ha*d t*rouble with the assignment.

19. That act is har*d to* follow.
20. He sag*ge*d and reele*d to*o much in the fir*st p*erformance.
21. We ha*d to* write a term paper.
22. Everyone ha*d to* wor*k to* complete it.

"DOUBLED" PLOSIVES. If you have one syllable ending with a plosive and the next syllable beginning with the same plosive, you do not have two stops but one, with the difference between a single consonant and a "doubled" consonant indicated by a lengthening of the time of the closure before the release in a plosion. In the word *bookcase*, for example, you do not stop and release the first / k / and then stop and release the second / k /. You obstruct the air stream with the back of the tongue as you would on a single / k /, but you hold the air stream closed off for a longer time before you release it. The same principle holds true even if the two plosives are in successive words. Note that *last time* is not pronounced the same as *lass time*, and *missed ten* differs from *Miss Ten*. There are two distortions associated with this principle against which you should guard. Careless speakers tend to treat doubled plosives as if they were single ones, and pedantic speakers tend to stop and explode each plosive in the pair.

Materials for Practicing Doubled Plosives

1. You ough*t to* vote in this election.
2. Hi*t to* center field.
3. I ha*te to* attend that class.
4. The coach will pic*k K*im for the award.
5. We ha*d d*ozens of offers of help.
6. We all hope to win the bi*g g*ame next week.
7. He dyed the ro*be b*rown.
8. What is a "hi*p p*erson"?
9. We had to be*d d*own in the back yard.
10. The children begged to go along, but they were turne*d d*own.

11. No one go*t to* look at it.
12. Can't you ta*ke K*evin with you?
13. I am looking for a ri*de d*owntown.
14. No honest player would rig games for profit.
15. I forgo*t to* pack clean shirts for the trip.
16. I pass*ed t*en cars before the crash.
17. He told me he could ty*pe p*erfectly.
18. Who would ro*b B*en of his last dollar?
19. All he had to do was qui*t to* prove his point.
20. Ma*d d*ogs and Englishmen go out in the noonday sun.

STOP-PLOSIVE FOLLOWED BY A NASAL. If a nasal consonant
follows a plosive, the air stream is obstructed by the articulators
for the plosive in the usual way, the closure is held for a moment while the velum drops down to open the passage to the
nose, and the air is then popped up through the nasal passages.
Be certain that you do not insert the vowel / ə / between the
plosive and the nasal, and be careful not to turn / pn / into
/ pm / and / kn / into / kŋ /.

Materials for Practicing Plosive Plus Nasal

/ pn /

1. Open the door, please.
2. How did it happen?
3. The entire torso of the sculpture seemed misshapen to me.
4. We had a wreck on the Tappen Zee Bridge.
5. We cleaned the canvas with turpentine.
6. It seemed a curious happenstance to me.
7. Does his firm have any openings I would be interested in?
8. The little fellow couldn't wait for the watermelon to ripen.
9. I bought it from the Upham Company.

/ kn /

1. My faith in human beings has been shaken.
2. He lives in Beacon, New York.

3. No one has reckoned the cost of the project.
4. The phonograph is broken and should be repaired.
5. I wakened to the sound of trumpets.
6. Why did he move to Hackensack?

/ dn /

1. He burst into the room suddenly.
2. This product was made in France.
3. Who let the snake into the Garden of Eden?
4. I have joined the Rod and Gun Club.
5. Auden is one of my favorite modern poets.
6. Why have you hardened your heart against me?
7. The dentist could not deaden the pain.
8. The entire university was saddened by the news.
9. It was the ship's maiden voyage.
10. Is that a symphony by Haydn?
11. It's too heavy a burden for you to bear.
12. Personally I think it's good riddance.
13. He had an answer for everything.
14. The judge refused to pardon him.

/ tn /

1. They threw rotten tomatoes at the speaker.
2. She was wearing a simple cotton dress.
3. Seton Hall hasn't lost a game this season.
4. The mailman was bitten three times last week.
5. Ill-gotten gains will do you no good.
6. Why haven't you written the report?
7. He appears to be smitten by her charms.
8. Farmers fatten up the hogs before slaughtering time.
9. Have you ever eaten rattlesnake? Certainly not!
10. Batten down the hatches!
11. Put on your hat and coat.
12. Who wants to buy a Siamese kitten?
13. Button up your overcoat.

14. The Titans are at the bottom of the league.
15. He wants to straighten this mess out.
16. The president has asked us to tighten our belts.

/ dnt /

1. You shouldn't have done that.
2. I couldn't care less.
3. He said he wouldn't go, but he did.
4. These shoes are wooden ones. Wouldn't you like to see them?
5. Are you sure they didn't like the play?
6. It's true I hadn't eaten frog legs before.
7. The doctor said we shouldn't eat mutton.
8. Everyone insisted he couldn't understand the assignment.
9. The instructor didn't believe them.
10. I could tell he hadn't practiced. Couldn't you?
11. I didn't hear the phone ring.
12. The adviser insisted that pledges shouldn't be beaten.
13. The mayor didn't listen to his party's bosses.
14. Wouldn't it be better to decide for yourself?
15. Aren't you afraid of rodents?
16. I hadn't thought much about it.
17. Couldn't you make up your own examples?

STOP-PLOSIVE FOLLOWED BY A LATERAL. When a lateral follows a homorganic stop-plosive, the air is released in an unusual way. The air is ploded over the sides of the tongue. To make the / tl /, for example, you place the tongue tip firmly on the gum ridge, hold the tongue tip firmly against the ridge, and pop the air over the sides of the tongue. Do not let the tongue drop between the / t / and / l /, because that will insert a vowel between the two consonants. The / tl / and / dl / are sound combinations, lateral plosions, and you should not conceive of them as being formed separately but together. There are two common distortions of these sound combinations: (1) incomplete closure, and (2) substitution of the glottal stop for the / t / in the / tl / combination. To produce a correct / tl / or / dl /, the tongue tip must touch the gum ridge and press firmly against the ridge until the combination is completed. The substitution of a stop-plosive made with the vocal folds for the first portion of the / tl / combination is rather common in the greater New York area. Check to be certain that in such words as *battle, bottle, total, futile,* and *mutilate* you make the sound with the tongue tip and not back in the throat.

Materials for Practicing / dl / and / tl /

1. Handle it with care.
2. He received five gold medals in one day.
3. How can you choose between Tweedledum and Tweedledee?
4. Paddle your own canoe!
5. The warden was accused of coddling the prisoners.
6. Is yodeling good for your voice?
7. The little toddler fell constantly.
8. We ate by candlelight.
9. I read a story about a headless horseman.
10. Oddly enough, he hit the wrong pedal on the organ.
11. I'm hoping to settle the case out of court.
12. I have a mutilated copy of my own.
13. We are studying the fundamentals of speech.
14. They used bottles for weapons in the street battle.
15. The subtleties of the story escaped him.
16. The children called the informer a tattletale.
17. The teacher did not think I was entitled to an A.
18. In Westerns, cattle rustlers are never gentlemen.
19. She threw a bottle of ink at me in a futile attempt to stop me.
20. They looked up the vital statistics in the Atlas.
21. Do not use a glottal stop in these exercises.
22. Every time I met Tom, he was hatless.
23. Myrtle is doing volunteer work at a mental hospital.

STOP-PLOSIVE FOLLOWED BY A FRICATIVE. When a fricative follows a stop-plosive, a firm closure is made for the plosive, the air pressure is built up at the point of closure, and the air is then released through the opening of the fricative. Check your pronunciation of the following words to be certain that you get a good firm closure on the plosive and a quick accurate release on the fricative: *rips, rates, rocks, ribs, raids, rugs.* You should also be sure that you have good vocal vibration on the voiced sounds / bz /, / dz /, and / gz /.

Materials for Practicing / ps / and / bz /

rips	ribs
ropes	robes
apes	Abe's
lopes	lobes
Epps	ebbs

1. How many cross-country trips have you taken?
2. We bought tubs and tubs of butter.
3. She hopes to become a star in Mr. Webb's movie.
4. It didn't take him long to learn the ropes.
5. The drapes are on fire.
6. All the tribes are constantly at war with one another.
7. Be sure to buy enough tubes of paint to finish the jobs.
8. He often rubs the lamp, but nobody appears.

/ ts / and / dz /

beets	beads
bets	beds
pats	pads
knots	nods
fates	fades
bites	bides
newts	nudes
hurts	herds

1. It's not a waste of time.
2. The boats are docked in the harbor.
3. That store sells many brands of paint.
4. Birds of a feather flock together.
5. It's what's up front that counts.
6. We heard many complaints in the courtroom.
7. God's in His heaven, all's right with the world.
8. By flanking the ends, our team can run complicated pass patterns.
9. The courts' dockets are crowded.
10. I hope she accepts my invitation.
11. The administration followed a "hands-off" policy.
12. The Boy Scouts' tents are on the front lawn.
13. The tax will finance new roads.
14. There are many pads in the wrestling room.
15. One faces many hazards on a safari.
16. His doubts are well-founded.
17. Her moods are constantly changing, because she broods over everything.
18. We want deeds, not words.
19. He lifts weights once a week at the gym.
20. There is more faith in honest doubt than in many creeds.
21. That's all. The period's over.
22. She writes home often when she needs money.
23. He meets his responsibilities, but he gets no credit for it.
24. There were no grounds for a good case.
25. I must check on the rates at the hotel.
26. Her hands are trembling. She waits for an answer.
27. Pangloss proved that this is the best of all possible worlds.
28. "What's time? Leave Now for gods and apes! Man has forever."
29. "The thoughts of men are widened with the process of the suns."
30. He reads all his assignments.
31. A gentleman is one who never inflicts pain.
32. He respects the rights of other human beings and aids those in need.
33. "All have a right to an equal share in the benefits and burdens of government."

Materials for Practicing / ks / and / gs /

lax	lags
leaks	leagues
picks	pigs
jocks	jogs
tucks	tugs

1. The little boy was throwing rocks at the neighbors.
2. He organized the teams into two leagues.
3. He seeks only to make his point clear.
4. Have you ever eaten fresh figs?
5. Both locks were broken.
6. Their fraternity lags behind the others in scholarship.
7. I'm told that he rigs every class election.
8. He is so nervous even the clock's ticks upset him!

TWO FRICATIVES. When two fricatives occur together, you must be sure to articulate both sounds and permit the air stream to come through the first closure before permitting it to come through the second. There are three dangers here: (1) omission of one of the consonants, (2) the addition of a vowel between the two consonants, and (3) unvoicing of voiced sounds.

Materials for Practicing / fs / and / vs /

1. One's beliefs are his own business.
2. Life's a vapor that quickly vanishes.
3. The safes were supposed to be burglarproof.
4. The roof's on fire!
5. Jerry loafs around the house all day.
6. He often reads from *Leaves of Grass*.
7. A good politician, he loves a difficult campaign.
8. She lives in an adjoining county.
9. Mark believes in miracles, but he never performs any.
10. He rants and raves over insignificant irritations.

Materials for Practicing / θs / and / ðz /

1. Authorities were unable to reach the youth's parents.
2. For your health's sake, you should stop drinking.
3. He accepts without question many incredible myths.
4. The material comes in various widths and lengths.
5. It is 99$\frac{44}{100}$% pure.
6. She bathes in goats' milk.
7. Are there any truths that are self-evident?
8. The dancer writhes six hours a night at the club.
9. Paths that are "untrod" are not paths at all.
10. Not even music soothes those savages.

SIBILANT FOLLOWED BY A PLOSIVE. When a plosive follows a sibilant at the end of a word, the sibilant is articulated in the usual way, and the stop-plosive must be fully closed. Unless a vowel immediately follows the plosive in the next word, the plosive will not be released with aspiration. There are two distortions associated with this combination: (1) omission of the stop-plosive, and (2) overaspiration of the release of the plosive. Although the plosive does not always explode in this combination, it always stops and the air stream is obstructed for a moment. During the time that the plosive is being articulated, of course, no air at all is emitted, and the time taken by the closure is necessary to indicate the presence of the plosive. Some speakers, in an effort to be precise, overarticulate the plosive in the combination, releasing the sound in a great puff of air. To most listeners, this sounds pedantic; we do not recommend it.

Materials for Practicing / sk /

1. I only ask for what is just.
2. The risk is too great for so small a reward.
3. He said it was carved from an elephant's tusk.
4. Mr. Fiske wore his uniform to the party.
5. Everyone had his own task to perform.

Materials for Practicing / sp /

1. The cookies were not crisp.
2. Have you detected a lisp in my speech?
3. No one told her that the clasp was not fastened.
4. A wasp sting can be very painful.
5. You could have heard the gasp ten miles away!

Materials for Practicing / st /

1. He lives in Westport.
2. She is the least beautiful of the sisters.
3. Roast pork is on the menu tonight.
4. The note is past due.
5. What is your worst problem in speech?
6. I want your best quality of merchandise.
7. I missed Carolyn in the crowd.
8. I haven't the least doubt we'll win.
9. The horse is now at the post position.
10. What is your next question?
11. The enemy was forced back by the advancing troops.
12. I disagreed with the last proposition.
13. I trust you will rest better tonight.
14. Voters crossed party lines to elect that candidate.
15. The famous journalist was almost blind.
16. The defendant was accused of blasphemy against God.
17. His taste buds must be dead.
18. It is a situation of the utmost gravity.
19. I attended the cast party with her.
20. They lost money on that investment.
21. You must go to the game next week.
22. They all cost more than I can afford to pay.
23. Conservatives do not trust "big government."
24. I must practice diligently and regularly.
25. You could list many more examples for practice.

Materials for Practicing / ʃt /

1. He was lashed to the mast.
2. Mashed potatoes are somewhat fattening.
3. She secretly wished for more, but said nothing.
4. He pushed his way through the crowd.
5. Several were crushed by the stampeding mob.

Consonant Clusters

PLOSIVE BETWEEN TWO CONTINUANTS. When a stop-plosive occurs between two continuants, you must take great care to make a firm and complete closure for the plosive. The plosive will not be released in an explosion, but will be released instead through the opening for the fricative which follows. The danger, of course, is that you will omit the stop-plosive altogether and combine the two continuants that remain. There should be an instant between the two continuant sounds when no air is emitted at all because the articulators have completely stopped the air stream to form the stop-plosive of the cluster. *Grafts*, for example, should not sound like *graphs*.

Materials for Practicing / fts /

1. Dick is studying arts and crafts at the college.
2. The posse is searching all the hay lofts in the county.
3. She lifts our spirits when she enters the room.
4. The Crofts plan to spend their honeymoon in the Virgin Islands.
5. The lawnmower left tufts of grass here and there.

Materials for Practicing / lts /

1. He tilts the machine every time he plays.
2. The coat was made from dozens of pelts.

3. The gold is stored in underground vaults.
4. Every sweet saying melts in her mouth.
5. Fearful of burglars, she always bolts the door.

Materials for Practicing / nts /

1. She put several new dents in the fenders today.
2. We bought six pints of sherbert for the punch.
3. One of the mints is in Denver.
4. At the party she performed unusual stunts.
5. The Senate consents more than it advises.

Materials for Practicing / sts /

Distinguish between the following pairs of words by making a firm closure between the two / s / sounds with the tongue tip on the gum ridge:

mass	masts
guess	guests
lass	lasts
Joyce	joists
Tess	tests
miss	mists
pass	past's
Bess	bests

East side, West side   last season, next season
first semester, last semester   most certain, least certain
best sort, worst sort

1. I want to take the test some other day.
2. The host spoke with all the guests.
3. Last season, I played on the varsity.
4. Next summer, I'm going to Europe.
5. It was the first star for which the captain looked.
6. The car almost started.
7. She raced six times and lost them all.

8. Our senator voted against Smith's proposal.
9. Increased governmental activity has characterized this past century.
10. On the way home, she passed several tall buildings.
11. We lost several games last season. Just suppose we had won!
12. He is the worst sort of rogue. You just missed seeing him.
13. That car cost several thousand dollars.
14. We must see them tonight.
15. I cannot insist Sam take the position.
16. Of all the employees, he is least secure.
17. It was the least suitable selection.
18. She passed seven courses in basket weaving.
19. I'm told that is the best sign.
20. Mine will be the last speech of the evening.
21. There are seven tests scheduled for tomorrow.
22. Kipling wrote his *Just So Stories* for his own children.
23. He kept the rest so as to raise the price.
24. They live on East Sixth Street.
25. List some other examples.
26. I must not waste so much time.
27. I spent most of my energy on the last series.
28. Forget past setbacks. Give your best service.

Materials for Practicing / ldz /

1. That sorority holds a meeting only once a month.
2. Ruthlessly he wields his power.
3. Our contractor builds each house to the owner's specifications.
4. The child's every whim is indulged.
5. A good leader welds a group into a cohesive unit.

Materials for Practicing / ndz /

1. He lends his name to every liberal cause that comes along.
2. The bands are massed for the parade.

3. Wallace is effective at predicting economic trends.
4. Blest be the tie that blinds!

Materials for Practicing / sks /

1. She asks every teacher the same question.
2. Who carves those symbols on the desks?
3. He refuses to take any risks at all.
4. Joyce never shirks her tasks.
5. The Rusks are an old, respected family in this community.

Materials for Practicing / sps /

1. My sister is afraid of wasps.
2. Wisps of smoke were visible on the horizon.
3. She grasps everything very quickly.
4. Cleopatra and the asps were bosom pals.
5. She said that malocclusion was the reason she lisps.

TWO PLOSIVES PLUS SIBILANT. To master these clusters, you should remember two things we have told you before: (1) when two plosives come together, the first is stopped, but not exploded, and then the second is stopped and exploded; and (2) when a stop-plosive and a fricative come together, a firm closure is made for the stop but the release is made through the opening for the fricative. If you combine these two principles, you will have no difficulty with these clusters. Be sure that you completely obstruct the air stream to form the first stop-plosive; then firmly stop the air column with the articulators to form the second plosive; and finally release the second plosive at the place of articulation of the sibilant. The / ts /, remember, is a combination, and there is only one release of the air on that combination; the / t / is released through the / s / position.

Materials for Practicing / kts /

Read the following pairs of words, being certain that you distinguish the first from the second by getting a good firm closure for both plosives:

ax	acts
tracks	tracts
packs	pacts
sex	sects
ducks	ducts

1. He tried to get all the facts before making a judgment.
2. The professor's wife corrects all the papers for him.
3. The reformers stood on the corner distributing tracts.
4. My partner deducts his gambling losses on his tax return.
5. The chain restricts my movement considerably.

Materials for Practicing / pts /

1. That fiend corrupts everyone with whom he has contact.
2. The orchestra performed excerpts from a number of longer works.
3. The crypts are beneath the church.
4. That clique disrupts every meeting of the fraternity.
5. I'm told that she accepts any invitation she receives.

SIBILANT PLUS TWO PLOSIVES. This cluster formation should offer you no difficulty if you have mastered the principle related to two consecutive plosives. The usual simplification of these clusters results from omission of the first of the two plosives and the combining of the two remaining sounds. In careless speech, then, *masked* becomes *massed* and *clasped* becomes *classed*. Listen to what some of your friends do to the word *asked,* and you will be more careful to articulate all the sounds of these clusters. As in any other combination involving two consecutive stop-plosives, the first stop-plosive is completely closed but does not explode, and the second both stops and explodes.

Materials for Practicing / skt /

1. She risked her reputation to come tonight.
2. I asked her a dozen times and always got the same reply.
3. All day at the beach we basked in the sun.
4. We attended every masked ball during Carnival.
5. That tremendous tusked animal came charging at us.

Materials for Practicing / spt /

1. I gasped in wonder at the sight.
2. She thrust her tongue between her teeth when she lisped.
3. He grasped my hand and welcomed me to the United States.
4. In her clenched hand she clasped the dollar bill.

THREE CONTINUANTS. Making the articulatory adjustments necessary to produce a cluster made up of three continuants requires flexibility and control, but you should have no difficulty adding the initial continuant if you mastered the production of two consecutive fricatives. The usual distortion of this cluster formation is the omission of the second continuant, so that *health's*, for example, rhymes with *else* and *fifths* rhymes with *if's*.

Materials for Practicing Three Consecutive Continuants

1. Three fifths of the class were extraordinarily gifted.
2. He had difficulty adding seven twelfths and nine sixteenths.
3. He said those strange chords were ninths and thirteenths.
4. Why does liquor come in fifths?
5. The variation in lengths made sorting easier.
6. Youths that get into trouble are not always delinquents.
7. How one breathes this polluted air and lives is a mystery!
8. The physician advised us to move West for our health's sake.
9. Not prelaw, but prewealth's his major.
10. Her strength's returning, but it has been a slow process.

CHAPTER 3

Meaningful Speech

THUS FAR, we have talked only in terms of improving your production of sounds, either in isolation or in their common combinations. You are aware, however, that you do not talk a sound at a time, and we must give some attention to words and thought groups.

Pronunciation

Pronunciation, the utterance of words, is composed of two elements: (1) the selection of sounds, and (2) syllabic stress. You can, then, mispronounce a word in two ways. Either you can use incorrect sounds in the word's formation, or you can put the stress on the wrong syllable.

Selection of Sounds. Because all of Chapter 2 dealt with sounds and their common distortions, this section is in a sense a review. We will look at the material in a slightly different way, however, by grouping the deviations into four types: (1) omissions, (2) additions, (3) distortions and substitutions, and (4) transpositions.

OMISSIONS. Leaving out sounds (remember that we are not talking about the letters of the words as they are spelled but the sounds of the words as they are pronounced) is one of the most common forms of mispronunciation. Consonants in the middle and at the end of the word, consonants in combinations, vowels between consonants, and the second of two vowels separated by a hiatus (a tiny pause to separate adjacent vowels into separate syllables) are often omitted in careless speech.

Pole for *polled*, *revant* for *relevant*, *satistics* for *statistics*, *packs* for *pacts*, *sport* for *support*, *prayed* for *parade*, *delcate* for *delicate*, *pome* for *poem*, and *rune* for *ruin* are all examples of this type of mispronunciation.

Haplology is the technical name for omission of entire syllables. We prefer to call this error "telescoping," because one syllable disappears inside another like one segment of a telescope inside the next one. This error is likely to occur when two syllables in a row contain the same sound. *Probably* may turn into *probly* and *constitution* into *constution*, for example.

ADDITIONS. You can also mispronounce a word by adding sounds. The *ng* confusion (see page 29) is an example of this error. Another, called the "intrusive r," rather common in the East, is the insertion of an / r / in place of a hiatus between vowels. We would encourage you to remove the excrescent / r / from "the idear of it" and "the lawr of the land." The addition of an / r / in the words *wash* and *Washington*, sometimes heard in the South and Middle West, is also substandard.

Spelling misleads some people into the addition of sounds. To pronounce a / b / in the word *subtle*, for example, is to mispronounce the word. Because we are used to having vowels between most consonants of separate syllables, some speakers insert a schwa between the final consonant of one syllable and the initial consonant of the next in such words as *athletic*. Of course, this is an error you should avoid.

DISTORTIONS AND SUBSTITUTIONS. Dentalization of lingua-alveolar consonants, unvoicing of voiced consonants, raising of the tongue on the *th* sounds, raising of / æ / and / aʊ /, retraction of / ɔ / and / aɪ /, nasalization, diphthongation, substitution of / ɪ / for / ɛ / or / n / for / ŋ /, and other distortions and substitutions have been discussed in detail in Chapter 2. It should be enough here to remind you that all these deviations in sounds result in mispronunciation.

TRANSPOSITIONS. Mispronunciation also results from reversing sounds or reversing letters. *Asked* should not become *axed,* nor *relevant* become *revelant. Perspiration* and *hundred* should not be pronounced *prespiration* and *hunderd.*

Syllabic Stress. In contrast with languages like French, where syllables receive level or equal stress, American English is characterized by differences in the amount of stress on syllables. Indeed, there are various levels of stress; some words may have syllables receiving primary, secondary, and tertiary stress. There are three factors involved in stressing a syllable: (1) increase in loudness, (2) higher pitch, and (3) longer duration. Misplaced stress may not only call attention to itself but it may change the meaning of the word. Many two-syllable words receive stress on the first syllable if they are used as nouns or adjectives and on the second if they are being used as verbs. *Present* and *perfect* are examples of such words. Stress in English tends to be recessive—it usually goes early in the word. For example, although the verb *compare* is stressed on the second syllable, the adjective *incomparable* is stressed on the second syllable (which is the fourth syllable from the end of the word). Note also the stress pattern in the words *fatigue* and *indefatigable, famous* and *infamous, pious* and *impious,* and *lament* and *lamentable.* Remember, however, there are many two-syllable words stressed on the second syllable; it is substandard to stress the first syllable in such words as *Detroit* and *because.*

Gradation of Vowels

Just as variation in syllabic stress is characteristic of English, so also is variation in the form of vowels. Indeed, the two are related. In unstressed syllables, the vowels are weakened. Most vowels in unstressed syllables are reduced to schwa, although / i / may become / ɪ / and / u / may become / ʊ /. The first syllable in the word *above,* for example, is not / æ / but / ə /; the vowel in the second syllable in the word *beautiful* may be either / ɪ / or / ə /; and the vowel in the first word of the infinitive *to be* may be either / ʊ / or / ə /.

There are a group of words, called *form words* (because they are necessary for the form or syntax of our sentences but not for the central ideas), which have both stressed and unstressed pronunciations. These words are articles, prepositions, conjunctions, auxiliary verbs, linking verbs, and pronouns. Since the meaning is implied in the word itself, no stress on the word is necessary— unless you intend to emphasize the implicit meaning and make it explicit. For example, the word *and* implies addition. If there is no reason to emphasize the concept of addition, you would use the weak form of the word; if, however, you wished to underscore that idea, you would use the strong form. In the phrase *bread and butter,* you would ordinarily use the weak form [n] for *and,* but if you wanted to emphasize the fact that adding butter was unusual, you would use the strong form [ænd].

Materials for Practicing Unstressed Forms

Articles

a   Have a ball. Run a risk. It's a game.
an   It's an old story. He's an eager applicant.
the   Here comes the bride. Where are the others? The team
         lost the final game. The orgy followed.

Prepositions

at   She collapsed at the dance. Meet me at nine o'clock.
for   Ask for an extra one. For goodness' sake, sing "Tea for
         Two."
from   It's a souvenir from Fort Knox. We work from dark to
         dawn.
into   The attorney is looking into the case. He will take it
         into court.
of   I'm not tired of school. It's the principle of the thing.
to   Are you ready to go? Give it to me.

Conjunctions

and	Life and death. A girl and a boy. Joy and pain. Forever and ever.
as	She's as pretty as a painting. It's almost as expensive!
but	But you said you would! Everyone's going, but no one's staying.
or	I want only one or two of them. You may take either or both.
than	There are more than I wanted. He said nothing other than that.

Auxiliary Verbs

am	I am speaking at the meeting. Then I am staying home.
are	We are reading *War and Peace*. Most are reading the *Classic Comic* version.
can	He can read Sanskrit. Do you know what she can do?
could	I could have performed all night. I wish I could go.
do	How do you do? Do you want to attend?
does	Does it work? When does she perform again?
had	He claimed he had already paid. The cashier had made a mistake.
has	He has been to the farm. John has learned his lesson.
have	We have seen him often. We should have gone.
must	You must practice. Russ thought he must leave early.
shall	We shall do our part. Where shall we go?
should	What should I do now? You should write other examples.
was	It was going well. Why was he suspected?
were	We were running all the time. They were provoked.
will	Who will take my place? Anyone will be able to do it.
would	I would rather do it myself. Why would they want a new one?

Linking Verbs

am	I am tired of these materials. I suppose I am too lazy to create my own.
are	We are ready for anything. They are hostile.

was   It was a serious matter. Nick was eager to stay.

were   They were happy to escape the ordeal. All of them were pawns in the power struggle.

Pronouns

he   How could he do it? I think he erred.

her   I gave her all I had. Someone told her the supply was limited.

him   Explain it to him. Make him pay his share.

his   You shouldn't have told his wife about it. She resented his running around.

some   I need some help. Give me some money.

that   He believed that he was perfect. Everyone else thought that he should be perfected.

them   I saw them at the bar. Take them home or find them a taxi.

us   Give us your number. She tried to ignore us.

you   I'm working, you know, at the grill. Have you looked for another job?

your   I'll take your place. Always do your best.

Assimilation

A change in a sound caused by the influence of a neighboring sound is called assimilation. Sounds are not produced in isolation in meaningful speech, and some sounds are regularly changed in certain contexts in order to make the flow of speech easier. Assimilation is not "sloppy speech"; rather, it is an attribute of socially acceptable speech patterns. Failure to use standard assimilations sounds affected and pedantic. Of course, omission of a number of sounds and assimilation of the sounds remaining is careless and substandard. / dɪdʒuit / is now acceptable for "Did you eat?" for example, but / dʒit / is what John Davenport in his delightful *New Yorker* article (June 8, 1949) calls "Slurvian."

Assimilation may mean either (1) absorption and incorporation, or (2) causing to resemble. Both definitions are relevant to a discussion of sound changes, because both full assimilation (incorporation of one sound into an adjacent sound) and partial assimilation (one sound becoming more like an adjacent sound) occur in American English. Pronounce the words *less sure* together, and you will see that the / s / has been fully assimilated or absorbed into the / ʃ /. On the other hand, note that you pronounce the word *sink* / sɪŋk / and not / sɪnk /. To become more like the / k /, the / n / has changed into / ŋ /—a partial assimilation.

Partial assimilations, which account for most of the sound changes in your speech, are classified into three types according to the direction of influence. If a sound influences the sound that follows it, the assimilation is called progressive; if a sound influences the sound which precedes it, the assimilation is said to be regressive; if two sounds influence each other to produce a third, the assimilation is reciprocal.

Progressive Assimilation. The past tense and plurals and possessives offer the best examples of progressive assimilation in English. After the vowel was dropped from the pronunciation of most words in the past tense, the tense was indicated by the voiced / d /. The words *planned, called,* and *leered* are pronounced / pland /, / kɔld /, and / liəd /. If the sound preceding the past tense ending is voiceless, however, progressive assimilation occurs and the / d / becomes / t /. Note that the words *passed, hoped, flunked, coughed,* and *lashed* all end in / t /. The same kind of assimilation takes place in forming plurals and possessives. The ending / z / is changed into / s / after voiceless sounds. Compare the pronunciation of *cubs* and *cups, beads* and *beets, pigs* and *picks, elves* and *elf's, sheathes* and *sheath's.* (The same kind of progressive assimilation also occurs in the third person singular of the present tense of the verb.)

Regressive Assimilation. We have observed before that some voiced sounds are slightly devoiced before voiceless sounds. Anticipating the sound that will follow, the speaker modifies the preceding sound. Another example, already noted briefly, is the changing of / n / to / ŋ / before / g / and / k /—particularly in the same syllable. *Sink, sank, flunk,* and *honk* all contain / ŋ / rather than / n /. When the letter *n* ends a syllable and the next syllable begins with / k / or / g /, there is a good deal of variation in the use of / n / and / ŋ /. Some of your friends may pronounce *banquet* / bænkwɪt / and others / bæŋkwɪt /, just as some may say / ɪnkʌm / and others / ɪŋkʌm / for *income*. The only principle that can be observed here is that when the letter *n* ends a syllable before a syllable beginning with / k / or / g /, the sound will usually be / ŋ / if the next syllable is unstressed and final in the word, as in the words *Congress* and *ankle.*

Reciprocal Assimilation. Two sounds may influence each other and produce a third sound in their place. / zj / may become / ʒ /, / sj / may become / ʃ /, / tj / may become / ʃ / or / tʃ /, and / dj / may become / dʒ /. Pronounce the words *vision, mission, action, actual,* and *gradual* to note the assimilations. To pronounce such words as *issue* and *education* as / ɪsju / and / ɛdjʊkeɪʃən / is considered pedantic in the United States.

Since we do not speak a word at a time, but blend our words together in successions of syllables called phrases or thought groups, assimilations may occur between words as well as within them. You may, in connected speech, have reciprocal assimilations in such phrases as *as you know, I miss you, eat your words,* and *would you.*

Conclusion

There are, of course, other elements of meaningful speech, which we have not been able to include in this handbook. We have included those aspects we thought most essential for our purpose of speech improvement. We have concentrated on mastering production of acceptable sounds (enunciation), on combining these sounds in their usual combinations, on sound changes, and on pronunciation. We are now ready to turn our attention to improvement of voice.

Voice Glossary

Assimilation nasality   The result of nasal resonance being carried over from the nasal sounds in a word to the neighboring nonnasal sounds.

Auditory feedback   The aural reception of one's speech as it reaches the ear immediately after speaking.

Aural   Pertaining to the ear.

Clavicular   A type of breathing involving the use of the clavicles or *collarbones* to raise the rib cage in inhalation.

Diaphragm   Dome-shaped muscle separating the thoracic cavity from the abdominal cavity.

Glottis   Opening between the vocal folds.

Gross abdominal muscles   Large muscles in the abdominal cavity used actively in the phase of exhalation for speech.

Hypertension   Excessive tension.

Hypotension   Insufficient tension.

Kinesthetic   "Muscle sense." One's perception of how the muscular action of his body feels.

Larynx   Voice box. The organ that houses the vocal folds.

Laryngeal tone   Tone initiated at the larynx as the vocal folds begin to vibrate in phonation.

Laryngopharynx   Throat area behind the larynx.

Muscle tonus   Adequate muscle tension for effective functioning of the muscle.

Nasopharynx   Extension of throat area behind the nasal cavity.

Pharynx   Throat area with three sections—laryngopharynx, nasopharynx, and oropharynx.

Phonation   The process of producing vocal tone as a result of breath being vibrated between the vocal folds.

Resonance   Amplification and modification of sound.

Resonators   Three areas for amplifying and modifying the basic laryngeal tone for speech—pharyngeal cavity, oral cavity, and nasal cavity.

Respiration   The process of breathing for life sustenance and for speech.

Support of tone   The use of the gross abdominal muscles to give a firm, steady push on emission of the breath stream in speaking.

Tactile   Pertaining to the sense of touch.

Thorax   The upper cavity of the torso of the body.

Trachea   The windpipe.

Velum   The soft palate.

Viscera   The soft organs of the body in the abdominal cavity.

CHAPTER 4

Introduction to
Voice Improvement

An Analysis of Vocal Quality

YOUR VOICE is the result of many coordinated processes working together efficiently. Air is exhaled from the lungs, vibrated in the "voice box" (larynx), and transformed into vocal tone. Your basic voice quality is the result of the normal functioning of the vibration of your vocal folds (phonation) and of the amplification and modification of that laryngeal tone in the resonating chambers of your head and throat (resonance). Differences in voices are as numerous as differences in people. Even though anatomically everyone uses the same organs to produce normal voice, the two factors of heredity and environment influence basic variations. This has been discussed in the Foreword to the Student.

Not to be minimized is a third factor influencing voice quality —your feelings or your emotions. Scholars look to the psychologists for information concerning man's behavior and the relationship of his behavior to his personality. Because your pattern of communication is "vocal behavior," voice improvement is necessarily involved with you as a person.

A fourth factor influencing these basic variations in voice quality is skill. Individuals vary in the degree of their control over the speech mechanism, and this variance in control produces perceptible differences in vocal output. You were born into your environment with your own individual degree of speech proficiency, but any native skill can be developed and extended. Under conditions that encourage the growing child to function productively in all areas—physically, intellectually, and emotionally—his speech proficiency should also progress. Far too frequently skill in this area is not encouraged at early ages and is even hampered. Previously we mentioned that you learned to speak as a result of a combination of factors. This basic speech pattern is the result of the influence of speech you heard in your home, your community and later your school. Your basic skill in speaking was determined primarily by your own physical capabilities (heredity) and by the surrounding environment. If the speech you heard in your formative years was not acceptable and if nothing was done to encourage you to make it acceptable, then the result today is probably unsatisfactory. Consider a possible situation—if the young child develops a lisp (and the reasons for this articulatory defect are highly complex) and the parents think "It's sweet," or perhaps are even unable to recognize the articulation problem, then the child's skill in speaking is hindered. If the vocabulary level in his home or in his community is of a low level, then the child's chances for learning to use a meaningful vocabulary can be hampered. More seriously, if the child grows up in a home where the attitude is "Speak when spoken to," or "Speak only when you have something important to say," then the child can develop serious psychological handicaps that can influence his communication pattern.

All of the above succinctly stated postulates that you learned your present speech pattern and that if in your formative years you were limited in acquiring the accompanying skills for good, acceptable speech, then now is not too late to attempt to change.

Developing Self-Awareness

In the following pages a very personal part of you will be considered—your voice. This voice is as distinctly yours as your religious beliefs, your political loyalties, your fingerprints. Because your "voice is you," any change, any improvement, is going to involve more than mechanics. Your voice reflects you in your many moods, your thinking, your behavior patterns—all those factors that add up to form your personality. In these pages you will be given the knowledge, the techniques, and the skills necessary for good voice production. Then you will be told how to use this "good" voice production. However, much of the value of all of this knowledge will be lost if you do not develop, as quickly as possible, self-awareness. This awareness refers specifically to your fluctuating physical conditions, your emotional states, and the day-by-day progress in your voice-improvement program. For instance, you will soon become aware that on days when you are fatigued your voice practice will be less effective. The very fact that you have less physical energy to expend is reason enough not to be able to practice. However, physical fatigue also affects your mental state, so the problem is compounded. Mentally, you are in no mood to work, and physically you are unable to work. Tired muscles do not respond easily to physical stimulation, so that if the muscles are forced to function in a particular manner, the result could be increased muscular tension. This hypertension would certainly not produce the desired vocal response. You will discover also that on days when you have experienced an emotional upset, voice practice might be practically worthless. The fact that your emotions affect your physical condition, your powers of concentration, and your attitudes— all of this contributes to a highly complicated picture of why you are unable to practice when you are tense, anxious, or worried. If you are emotionally upset, your body reacts—your breathing is affected, muscles become tense, and coordination of muscular action is hampered. Concentration during this period is almost impossible, because your thoughts are on your worries. Your attitude toward the practice session will either be "I couldn't care less" or "I'm going to acquire this skill—or else." In this highly charged atmosphere, either attitude could obviously interfere seriously with productive practice.

On the brighter side, however, you will become sensitive to days that are potentially good for voice work. These days can be interpreted only on a highly individual basis. For some of you it will mean days when you are physically well and emotionally at ease. For others, it will mean days when attitudes are optimistic. Whatever the conditions, you can encourage profitable vocal practice on days when the vocal mechanism is functioning well (for example, no colds, hoarseness, or allergy irritations) and when mental concerns are minimal. Remember, such days do not always just "happen." More often than not they must be encouraged to happen.

We have referred frequently in this handbook to the psychological involvements in the speech process. At this point, we would like to assure you that not all changes in attitude and in application are spontaneous or deliberate. You may be a person who feels very hostile in the initial stages of the improvement program. Do not force yourself to reconsider or to reevaluate your feelings or position immediately. Let knowledge, time, and experience help you on the way to self-acceptance.

Auditory Acuity

An effective voice-improvement program is multifocused. The following are necessary considerations in such a program:

1. An awareness and a knowledge of the voice problem itself.
2. A willingness to change or improve your present voice.
3. A resolute attitude toward a planned-practice program.

Usually a person is made aware of a voice problem after a voice analysis or a voice evaluation has been made by a qualified teacher or clinician. Sometimes a person himself becomes aware of his voice problem because of physical discomfort, or because of remarks made by friends, or simply because he has heard a recording or taping of his voice. The important thing is for you to learn to recognize the *exact* sound of your voice. You should try to develop as quickly as possible *acuity of auditory feedback* —or the ability to hear your own voice accurately. This is really another form of self-awareness. This particular kind of self-awareness is related to your ability to analyze your present method of producing voice and to your sensitivity to the changes in your voice production as you try new vocal techniques. Before you can improve your voice you must learn to *listen*. Remember, your voice will improve in direct proportion to how much you *hear* of your voice problem. Become "voice" or "sound" conscious.

How well are you able to discriminate vocal sound at this early stage? Experiment with the following suggestions:

1. Face a corner wall of a carpeted room. Cupping a hand behind each ear, pull the ears slightly forward and begin to speak into the corner. The voice which reaches your ears will be fairly close to the voice which other people hear. Become acquainted with it.

2. Have a "new listening experience" the next time you listen to your favorite disc jockey or television program. Can you *put into words* the descriptions of the voices you are hearing?

It might be a good idea to take a close look at some of the factors that will specifically aid you in your improvement program. In the acquisition of any skill it is wise to take advantage of your senses—the visual, tactile, aural, and kinesthetic. As you practice the suggested voice exercises in this handbook look at yourself in a mirror (visual) and note how the articulators are moving. Are they active? Is the lower jaw too rigid? Are the back teeth clenched? Using your hand, spread the thumb and middle finger to cover the lower jaw area. Feel (tactile) the muscular action of the jaws and the muscular action under the lower jaw bones. Is this area hypertense? Too lax? Along with the visual and tactile approach, take advantage of the kinesthetic (muscle) sensations you experience as you practice. As you feel the muscular action tactually, close your eyes and try to perceive that muscular action. Can you recognize *how it feels?* Now you are ready to encourage the aural sense.

Momentarily pause and try the following suggestions to help you check on *how well you hear your own voice:*

1. Think for a moment—does your voice sound like the voice of anyone in your home? An indication of this would be the fact that you are frequently mistaken on the telephone for another member of your family. If this happens to you, then be assured that your voice has some aspects of the other person's voice quality. Listen to the voice of this person. Do you like the quality? If so, why? If not, why not?

2. Record your own voice. Deliberately use it in different emotional settings—anger, pleasure, surprise. What differences in the sound of your voice do you hear? What accounts for the vocal differences—the sound of your voice, or the words you are saying, or a combination of both factors?

Aural acuity will develop in a very specific way. In the initial stages of improvement you will be able to discriminate to a degree. You might become discouraged because you feel that the aural is of no help to you because seemingly you cannot discriminate at all. The best advice is to be patient, because in due time you will become sensitive to sound discrimination. The first person in whom you will be able to recognize deviations of speech will be your friend, classmate, parent, anyone—except yourself. You will so sharpen your discriminatory ability in this respect that your former favorite announcer or TV personality will begin to annoy you with his speech faults. The next stage of progress will refer to you directly. You will begin to hear yourself *after* you have made the error in articulation or after you have started to produce voice incorrectly—all too late because the sounds have been produced. This is the most frustrating stage of all. The next stage of development is most encouraging. As you start to speak you will have begun to change (as a result of continued practice) the involved muscular action to such a degree that you are able to *initiate* the pattern correctly. Now you are well on the way to permanent speech improvement. At this point do not be concerned about criteria in the use of your senses. You will be advised about these as you are introduced to the new vocal skills.

Practice Sessions

Basically, voice improvement involves retraining of muscle action, but you must not force this action. Rather, you must firmly encourage the desired muscular response. It should be obvious that this kind of practice must not be continued for any long span of time. Muscles used in a new or different manner tend to fatigue, and long periods of practice can prompt varied reactions. One of these reactions is related to aural fatigue. When you undertake your new voice-improvement program, your aural feedback will be unreliable. As you practice, you will be able to detect some changes in the quality of your voice, but the ability to discriminate will be short-lived. As you attempt a new technique, aurally and kinesthetically, you will be aware of differences, but if the muscles tire and revert back to their old pattern of movement (tired muscles tend to do exactly this), it is doubtful that you will notice that the voice produced is your "old" quality. Short periods of practice help to avoid this danger. In the beginning work about ten minutes at a time, but plan on frequent periods of practice. Short but repeated periods of work are highly beneficial. Plan on *daily* practice, because skipping days between sessions only retards your progress. Also, be inventive about your time to practice. Do not rely on an allotted "hour" for voice-improvement skills, because this time seldom materializes. Rather, make use of odd periods during the day. Practice in your car while driving to work or driving to school; practice as you walk across campus; practice as you dress in the morning or before you retire (if you are not too fatigued). It is better to plan for a specific time to try a new skill, but the reinforcing of that skill can be done during odd periods of the day. Whatever your approach, it is important for you to *progress* in your voice improvement. Do not allow intermittent practice periods to be responsible for spasmodic progress. Relearning and retraining can be the beginnings of boredom and dissatisfaction.

From this handbook you should acquire the skill necessary for the control and manipulation of three important components of voice production. Emphasis will be placed on the processes of resonance (oral, nasal, pharyngeal), breathing (respiration), and adequate tension of the vocal folds (laryngeal tension). Your voice-improvement program will first include a consideration of the development of correct and adequate vocal resonance. It is important that you are made aware of the necessity of having a "place for the voice to go" once the tone leaves the larnyx. The vibrated air must not be caught in hypertense chambers. This handbook concentrates on a somewhat unorthodox approach to voice production by deliberately considering resonance before respiration. The authors feel that because you have worked on

your articulation, which usually helps to develop a balance between nasal and oral resonance in articulation and therefore results in a balance of resonance in your voice quality, work in
voice improvement should take advantage of your acquisition of
this particular skill. With this in mind, the progression of acquisition of skills so vital to effective voice production will be
developed in this handbook in the following order:

1. Achievement of relaxed resonating cavities.
2. Development of correct respiration habits and the control of
   the muscular action that supports the outgoing breath stream.
3. Acquisition of adequate tension in the vocal folds.

In the Foreword there was reference to the limitations of this
text as a guide to voice improvement. A handbook is not detailed
and expansive enough in scope to include material for the correction of severe "clinic" voice cases. We will consider only those
defects of voice that are found in the habitual quality of speakers. Specifically, the voice types that are treated in this handbook
are strident, throaty, nasal (hypernasal and hyponasal), thin,
breathy, harsh, and hoarse.

CHAPTER 5

Resonance

Vocal Resonance

YOUR VOICE is produced in the larynx, which is commonly referred to as the Adam's apple. The larynx, about the size of a walnut, rests on top of the trachea (windpipe) and is composed of one bone, cartilages, and membranous tissues. The bone is to the larynx what the basketball hoop is to the net extending from it. The hyoid bone is at the top of the larynx, and from this bone extends the cartilaginous framework. The two cartilages that compose the framework are the thyroid cartilage and the cricoid cartilage. (*See* Figure 5–1.) The vocal folds are housed within the larynx and are attached at the front of the larynx just under the notch of the thyroid cartilage, the larger of the two cartilages. The folds stretch across the larynx and are attached at the rear to two small pryamid-shaped cartilages, the arytenoids. The opening between the folds is called the *glottis*, through which passes the exhaled breath stream as it is emitted from the trachea. The vocal folds open and close with a rhythmic motion that is the result of two forces—innervation by the laryngeal nerve and air pressure. At the present time the most widely accepted theory of the abduction of the vocal folds is the myoelastic —aerodynamic theory. This theory relates the movement of the muscles of the larynx (myo = muscle; elastic = movement) to the force of the exhaled air (aero = air; dynamic = force). This theory postulates that when the air pressure (exhaled breath

123

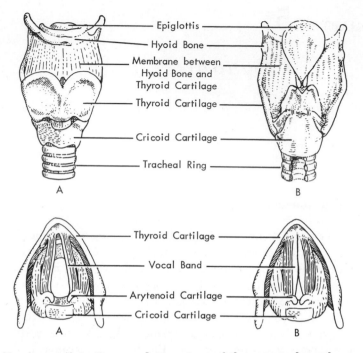

Epiglottis
Hyoid Bone
Membrane between
Hyoid Bone and
Thyroid Cartilage
Thyroid Cartilage
Cricoid Cartilage
Tracheal Ring
A   B

Thyroid Cartilage
Vocal Band
Arytenoid Cartilage
Cricoid Cartilage
A   B

FIGURE 5-1. Front and rear views of the principal cartilages
of the larynx and diagrammatic representation of the vocal folds
showing attachments to cartilages of the larynx. Illustration
redrawn with permission of the Macmillan Company from BASIC
SPEECH, 2/e, by Eisenson and Boase. Copyright © The Macmillan Company, 1950, 1964.

stream) beneath the vocal folds equals the muscular pressure
that holds the folds together, the folds are forced open. Along
with this movement there is innervation by the tenth cranial
nerve, the vagus nerve. The laryngeal branch of this nerve specifically innervates the vocal process. The vibration of the folds
gives your voice its fundamental vocal tone or basic laryngeal tone.
This laryngeal tone is influenced by the physical structure of your
larynx and is established by two actions: (1) by the vibration of
the outgoing breath stream, and (2) by the amount of tension
within the muscles of the larynx and within the vocal folds them-

selves. The entire process of producing voice is termed *phonation* from the Greek word φωνή, meaning *a sound*. This basic sound is then amplified in the pharyngeal cavity, and the process of resonance is initiated.

Resonance may be defined as the amplification and modification of sound. Resonance of voice simply means the development and reinforcement of the basic laryngeal tone as it leaves the larynx. This tone is originally a rather weak one and needs to be amplified. The amplification takes place in three cavities—the pharyngeal, oral, and nasal. (*See* Figure 5–2.) All three kinds of vocal resonance are necessary for good voice production. Pharyngeal and oral resonance help to increase the mellow, rich

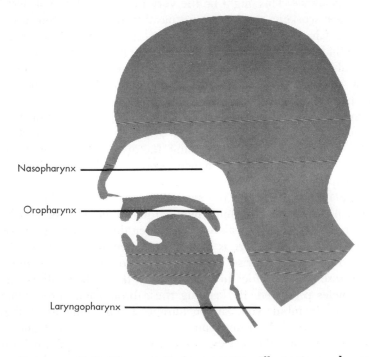

Nasopharynx

Oropharynx

Laryngopharynx

F I G U R E 5–2. The principal resonators. Illustration redrawn with permission of the Macmillan Company from THE IMPROVEMENT OF VOICE AND DICTION, 2/e, by Jon Eisenson. Copyright © The Macmillan Company, 1965.

tones of your voice. Nasal resonance, apart from being needed in the production of the nasal consonants of American English (see Chapter 2, page 26), is necessary to give your voice quality needed brightness.

The resonance system is so structured that what affects one resonance chamber necessarily affects, to some extent, the other two chambers. If you are working on developing good oral resonance, which demands an open, enlarged oral cavity, with lower jaws relaxed and back teeth unclenched, the physical structure itself of the mouth will force the soft palate (velum) up against the back pharyngeal wall during this practice. This kind of movement of the velum often closes off the nasal passages and eliminates nasal resonance. This might be the very physical action you want if you are working on eliminating nasality or assimilation nasality (see Chatper 6, page 132). Therefore the student must be aware that concentration on improving one kind of resonance will noticeably improve the resonance process in general. However, for a clearer understanding of resonance in voice production, the three kinds will be considered separately.

Physics of sound demonstrates that the shape of the resonator, the size of its opening to the outer air, and the surface texture of the resonator are all influencing factors in determining the quality and amount of resonance produced. Because the size and shape of your nasal, oral, and pharyngeal cavities can be manipulated and because the size of the openings of these cavities can be varied, the fundamental tone of your voice can be reinforced. Generally speaking, the larger the resonating cavity, the more resonation there is of the fundamental tone and of the lower overtones. Likewise, within limits, the larger the openings of the resonating cavities to the outer air, the higher will be the frequencies produced. By keeping these basic sound-production principles in mind, you can encourage a more mellow, fuller, and vibrant voice by using your resonators effectively. Concentrate on enlarging the pharyngeal and oral cavities and work for increased lip-and-jaw movement. The third factor to keep in mind is that of the influence of surface texture on vocal resonance. Tension in the resonating cavities resulting in rigid chamber wall "texture" minimizes a mellow voice. Relaxation of these cavities is necessary and desirable. Sounds reverberated off hard surfaces do not benefit from the cushion effect of soft surfaces, where the unpleasant sounds are dampened.

Kinds of Resonance

Pharyngeal Resonance. The pharyngeal cavity probably contributes most of the resonance to your voice quality simply because of the anatomical position of the larynx. The pharynx (throat) can be conveniently divided into three areas, the laryngopharynx, the oropharynx, and the nasopharynx. These divisions indicate that the pharynx extends from the area where the larynx is located, running upward behind the nasal cavity. (The back pharyngeal wall is closely related to the effective functioning of the various resonance areas.) Because of the anatomical relationship of the larynx to the pharynx (laryngopharynx) the fundamental laryngeal tone can be reinforced immediately upon production when the tone is at its strongest. It is of extreme importance that the pharyngeal muscles be neither too tense nor too lax but that they have what is called adequate *muscle tonus.* This means that the muscles should have just enough firmness, just enough "tone," to encourage the right amplification.

FAULTS OF INADEQUATE PHARYNGEAL TENSION. If the muscles of the walls of the pharyngeal cavity are too tense, as the fundamental tone of the voice is resonated in this area, the quality of the voice can become *strident.* (There is usually accompanying tension in the other resonators.) A strident voice sounds thin (lacking lower overtones), pinched, and strained, and it is normally high-pitched. When the voice is low-pitched, the faulty quality is usually termed *raspy.* This latter problem also has the accompanying condition of hyperlaryngeal tension, which will be discussed in Chapter 7.

Too-lax muscular action in the laryngopharynx results in minimal pharyngeal resonance, and this can encourage a *throaty* quality or a thick-sounding voice. Other factors, however, can contribute to this problem of throatiness—one functional and the other organic. Along with the lax pharyngeal muscular action can be too little movement of the tongue. Because the lowest muscle fibers of the tongue are attached to the hyoid bone of the larynx, limited movement of the tongue can negatively influence voice quality. Organically, enlarged tonsils can be a very concrete factor in contributing to this unpleasant voice. Obviously, a doctor should be consulted first for appropriate treatment. However, the throaty quality does not always just disappear after medical care. Frequently the student has acquired speech patterns that have developed as factors accompanying the medical problem (for example, heavy, lax movement of the tongue), and because the speech production has since become habitual, the student will need to work to improve the quality of his voice despite the alleviation of the medical condition.

Exercises

For the best possible pharyngeal resonance keep in mind a relaxed lower jaw and a relaxed oral cavity. The latter is especially important because the back wall of the laryngopharynx leads into the oral cavity. If the oral cavity is tense, the back pharyngeal wall becomes tense, and vice versa. The following exercises are important in helping you to determine the exact kinesthetic and tactual sensations of hypertension versus relaxation.

For the strident or raspy voice (relaxed resonators are important):

1. Upon inhalation of breath, give a wide yawn, and as you exhale the breath, initiate the sound of / a / and sustain the sound as you terminate the yawn with closed lips. Repeat a few times, concentrating on a relaxed lower jaw.

2. Repeat the above exercise using the following variations:
    a. Spread your hand across your throat, with the thumb and middle finger touching just under the jaw bones. Initiate the yawn, and try to feel (tactual approach) the looseness in the lower jaws and relaxation of the muscles in the laryngopharyngeal area.
    b. Close your eyes—repeat the exercise and try to sense how the muscular action feels (kinesthetic).

For the throaty voice (precise movement of the articulators is important):

1. Use the above exercises, but instead of initiating an / a / sound upon exhalation, practice the following sets of sounds, making a firm contact on the alveolar ridge with the tip of the tongue.
   a. ta-ta-ta-ta, etc.
   b. da-da-da-da, etc.
   c. la-la-la-la, etc.
   d. na-na-na-na, etc.

   Make sure that there is no hypertension in the jaw bones as the tongue tip is raised to the alveolar ridge during these exercises. You may do all of the sounds on one exhalation or use a separate breath for each set of sounds. Precise and sharp movements of the front part of the tongue are an important asset in improving a throaty quality.

Oral Resonance. As a result of your work in the beginning chapters of this text you acquired correctness and clarity of articulation. In the process you became aware of the necessity of moving your articulators. The term *oral activity* is used to designate this skill. You found that the tongue tip was capable of reaching up and touching the alveolar ridge for the t–d–n–l sounds of American English. In the production of the / aɪ / and / aʊ /, you discovered that the tongue and lip positions had to be modified if these sounds were to be made without deviations. You also found that many sounds were produced with more accuracy and clarity when you opened the oral cavity and worked for a relaxed lower jaw and opened back teeth. You discovered that a tight jaw was to be avoided. Whether you were aware of it or not at the time, you were developing a very important aspect of good voice quality—oral resonance. Because the oral cavity can be more easily manipulated than the other two resonating cavities, your voice-improvement program should rely heavily on this factor. Because effective oral resonance depends on how the oral cavity is used, you should concentrate on good control in this area.

It may be noted that oral resonance is so basic to voice production that it can be said to be a necessary component of every

characteristic of voice. Conversely, lack of adequate oral resonance contributes to most of the types of defective qualities of
voice—throatiness, stridency, raspiness, thinness, and nasality.

FAULTS OF INADEQUATE ORAL RESONANCE. If you are
told that you have a voice quality that lacks oral resonance, this
means very simply that the fundamental laryngeal tone of your
voice is not receiving enough amplification in the oral cavity.
When this happens in voice production the result is usually a
thin voice, or what is commonly known as a "little girl's voice"
(or a "little boy's voice"). Resonance in the oral cavity amplifies
the lower, more mellow overtones and plays a major part in determining the identifying overtones of the vowels in American
English. A very broad, general definition of a vowel has been
given as "a sound produced without obstruction of the breath
stream." The authors agree that the definition is accurate—as far
as it goes. However, if you stop at this point in the definition, the
immediate intellectual reaction would be, "Then why do vowels
sound differently? What makes it possible for us to identify an
/ a / from an / i / sound?" The difference is governed by the
modification of the articulators as the unobstructed breath stream
is allowed to escape. Using your mirror, watch the movements
of your mouth as you produce a prolonged / a / sound and then
a prolonged / i / sound. Note the change in tongue placement,
lip position, and tension of the jaws. If the modification of the articulators is necessary for the exact placement of the vowels,
then you can also become aware of what happens to the resonance within the oral cavity as the articulators change position.
This amplification and modification of the tone within the oral
cavity produces the identifying differences of sound among the
vowels of our language.

In addition, this modification and amplification of tone has a
meaningful effect on your voice quality. Because you have
worked on opening your mouth by lowering your jaw and unclenching your back teeth, you are allowing the lower, richer
tones to develop—aided, of course, by relaxation in this area.
This approach will make a marked difference in your *thin* voice.
Automatically your voice will become more resonant, fuller, and
"older" (more mature). *Do not manipulate your pitch level.*

Even though a thin voice is usually high-pitched, lowering the pitch is not a lasting solution. It can, in fact, be injurious if not handled with extreme caution. One of the basic theories of good voice production with which we concur is that a voice produced correctly will usually seek its own optimum pitch level. Only in rare cases does pitch have to be deliberately manipulated. If you have good habits of respiration for speech which result in a well-supported, steady stream of exhaled air, your vocal folds will vibrate effectively. Correct and effective vibration of the vocal folds is a fundamental factor in maintaining a dependable pitch range.

Exercises

Before you begin to work toward improvement in oral resonance, it would be helpful for you to review how the vowels are produced in your language. Return to Chapter 2 of this handbook and consult the pages on the descriptions of the vowels. Note particularly which vowels are lax and which are tense. For example, you will find that the / i / is a high, front, tense vowel, whereas the / ɪ / is a slightly lower, front, lax vowel. That term *tense* does not mean "hypertense." Oral resonance is frequently less effective because the tense vowels are produced with hypertense muscular action of the articulators.

For the throaty, strident, or raspy voice:

1. Using Figures 2–4, 2–5, and 2–6 in Chapter 2 as a guide, move from high to low vowels, beginning with the front vowels, and try to produce all of the vowels with a similarity in voice quality. Do not allow the necessary tongue tension demanded to produce some of the vowels to interfere with your attempt to acquire sameness in voice quality. (Tense vowels demand tension in the tongue for their correct production.)

2. Count from one to ten. Say the numbers with a similarity of oral and pharyngeal resonance—for example, do not allow the number three to sound tight and pinched because of the tense vowel / i /.

3. Use the diphthongs of American English, and let the sounds reverberate in the oral cavity by prolonging each element of the diphthong as you say them. Get a "round" feeling inside the oral cavity by unclenching your back teeth and having a relaxed lower jaw as you initiate the first element of the diphthong.

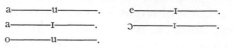

4. Return to Chapter 2, and using all of the practice material in the sections on the diphthongs, work for a relaxed throat, open oral cavity, unclenched back teeth, and flexibility of tongue.

For the nasal voice:

(See the following section on nasal resonance.)

Nasal Resonance.   Nasal resonance is a necessary component of good voice quality. Breath vibrated by the vocal bands and resonated in the nasal cavity contributes a brightness or brilliance to the human voice. Proof of this can be found when one has a cold and nasal resonance is either minimized or restricted entirely. The result is a muffled, dull vocal quality, actually a quality that can interfere with intelligibility of speech. Because the cold has irritated the membranous tissue in the nasal cavities, you are unable to breathe through your nose and therefore unable to resonate in these cavities. This lack of nasal resonance specifically causes the distortion or substitution of the / m /, / n /, and / ŋ / sounds. These three sounds depend on nasal resonance for their production. Thus the phrase *Good morning* can become *Good bordig.* From your study of sound production and placement, the substitutions in the above phrase should be obvious: / b / as a bilabial plosive sound replaces the bilabial nasal / m /, the lingua-alveolar plosive / d / replaces the lingua-alveolar nasal / n /, and the velar plosive / g / replaces the velar nasal / ŋ /.

From your work in articulation and from concentration on developing oral resonance, you must now be conscious of the involvement of the soft palate both in the production of articulated sounds and good voice. You must now be able to recognize the deliberate movement of this part of the oral cavity as you produce nasal sounds and as you try to achieve an "open" oral cavity for improved oral resonance in your voice. At this point take a minute to reinforce the kinesthetic sensation.

1. Using a mirror for visual assurance, open your mouth wide, trying for an open throat, and inhale a large amount of air. Gasp *inwardly*, with a prolonged intake of breath. You will experience a "drafty" sensation inside the mouth and you will see the velum move upward and then immediately relax with a downward motion. Repeat several times—slowly.

2. Now quicken the pace. Using the mirror again with the same physical positioning of the mouth and throat, pant hard on an *intake* of breath, repeating rapidly. The velum will move vigorously. You can be assured of this action by the quick, jerky movements of the uvula, which terminates the soft palate.

3. To reinforce the visual and kinesthetic sensations in the movement of the soft palate, try the following: use the mirror to note the opening and closing of the nasopharyngeal area as you pronounce a prolonged / ŋ / sound followed by a prolonged, relaxed / a / sound.

/ ŋ /————/ a /————/ ŋ /————/ a /———— *Repeat*.

Note how the velum lowers on the / ŋ / sound and perceptibly raises on the / a / sound.

FAULTS OF INADEQUATE NASAL RESONANCE. Before exploring faults of inadequate nasal resonance, we need to define some terms. *Nasality* pertains to the negative aspect of nasal resonance and falls into two types, *hypernasality* and *hyponasality*. *Hypernasality* refers to excessive nasal resonance in the voice, and *hyponasality* or *denasality* refers to insufficient nasal resonance in the voice. A third term, *assimilation nasality*, also belongs to this group of resonance defects even though it more specifically involves the distortion of the articulated sounds in your speech. All three faults are directly related to the inaction of the velum.

In the production of effective nasal resonance the velum moves downward, allowing the exhaled breath to be resonated in the nasal cavity. This nasal resonance is imperative in the production of the three nasal sounds of / m /, / n /, / ŋ /. Hypernasality results when the velum remains lowered during the production of the other sounds in American English and no physical movement is made to close off the opening to the nasal cavity. The entire speech pattern is then colored with excessive nasal resonance. Conversely, if during speaking, the velum remains in the position of closing off the nasal cavity so that even the nasal sounds are not allowed the necessary resonance in the nasal cavity, the voice quality is then hyponasal or denasal.

Assimilation nasality involves the presence of nasal resonance in sounds that do not demand nasal resonance for their production. The word *assimilation* comes to us from the Latin *ad similare*, meaning to "take into," "to affect." In this problem, a word containing a nasal sound is completely nasalized. Instead of the nasal sounds alone having nasal resonance, the nasal sounds "take into themselves" or "affect" the neighboring sounds so that other sounds in the word are tinged with nasal resonance. Again, the solution is the conditioning of the velum. It must be made to function actively—that is, the muscular action of the velum must be controlled so that it moves downward for all nasal sounds, allowing for nasal resonance, and then moves upward and back against the pharyngeal wall for all of the other sounds in the word.

There is a special nasality problem called *nasal twang*. It is simply hypernasality compounded with tension in the back pharyngeal wall. The voice quality assumes, in addition to excessive nasal resonance, a pinched, tight sound—a "twang." Adequate nasal resonance and particularly relaxation of the oral cavity are helpful solutions to this kind of problem.

Exercises

1. Using a tactual and kinesthetic approach, reinforce your awareness of nasal resonance in the nasal cavity. Place your thumb and forefinger over the bridge of your nose and say a prolonged / n / sound, and then change your tongue position for a prolonged / l / sound. Note the vibration in the nasal cavity on the / n /. There should be no nasal vibration on the / l /.

2. The following sentences may be used for both hypernasality and hyponasality by stressing the appropriate sentences. If you have hypernasal resonance, use the sentences in pairs. Listen carefully to the sentences with the nasals in them, feeling (tactile) the vibration in the nose as you stress and prolong the words with nasal sounds in them. Do not allow the nasal resonance of the nasal sounds to carry over to the neighboring nonnasal sounds. The sentences with no nasal sounds in them should have only minimal vibration in the nasal cavity (if any at all). If you have hyponasality, spend more time on the sentences with nasal sounds in them—prolonging the nasals for increased nasal resonance.

   a. The nine men on the team demanded a new decision from the umpire.

   b. The five players asked for a rest period.

   c. Can you imagine having only candy for lunch?

   d. Her favorite period of the day is right after breakfast.

   e. Lying on the sand under the burning sun can be dangerous to one's complexion.

   f. Wait for Bill to go with us to the beach.

   g. In American English the vowels and diphthongs are seemingly more often influenced than the consonants are by neighboring nasal sounds.

   h. Do you suspect that this is probably true?

3. For the improvement of assimilation nasality try the following pairs of words. Stress the vowels before the nasal sounds, and then make a concerted effort to have nasal resonance *only on the nasal sounds.*

at	an
abbey	Aunty
attitude	amplitude
cat	can
it	in
lit	linen
settle	sentinel
cow	now
sow	sound
I	nine

For variation put the pairs of words into sentences—for example:

a. *At* the World's Fair I noticed *an* attitude of friendliness among the visitors.
b. Westminster *Abbey* will never be the same after *Aunty* Mame's visit last summer.

CHAPTER 6

Respiration

PERHAPS the process most vital to the production of human speech is respiration. The entire process has two phases—inhalation and exhalation. The purposes of respiration are twofold: (1) you breathe for your very life's existence, and (2) you breathe for the production of speech. In breathing for life, the combined phases take anywhere from three to five seconds and are about equal in duration. This means that the amount of air taken in by the lungs in inhalation is about equal to the amount of air expelled in exhalation. Also, the phase of inhalation, which brings fresh oxygen to your body, is an active phase, whereas exhalation, which expels the waste products from your body, is passive. Actually, exhalation is nothing more than relaxation following the contraction of the necessary muscles in inhalation. The entire process is involuntary and is controlled by the brain stem, which is the core of the brain, essentially an extension of the spinal cord (through which all nerve impulses are channeled) —specifically the medulla. Proof of the involuntary nature of this act can be found in the incident of the young infant who holds his breath in anger while the nervous parents stand by helplessly. Their fears are needless, because the infant can voluntarily control the breathing process only for a limited time. As soon as there is enough accumulation of carbon dioxide in his blood stream, the infant will black out, and immediately the involuntary breathing pattern will resume. Breathing for speech is slightly different from breathing for life. The most important difference is the fact that in exhalation the breath is controlled voluntarily while it is being expelled slowly or quickly, depending on the needs of the speaker. A second difference is that the breathing pattern for life sustenance is even and smooth, whereas in speech the respiration takes on the tempo of your thoughts and feelings. As you express your ideas, your breathing pattern is determined by your grouping of the words used to explain your thoughts. This rhythm pattern is further influenced by your feelings at the moment of utterance. If you are angry, your voice will probably be used more forcefully, with a jerky rhythm, hence demanding more breath. If you are in a relaxed mood, the flow of breath might even be as smooth in rhythm as it is in breathing for life. In any event, the important point is that breath for speech is voluntarily controlled and that the period of exhalation is usually longer than the period of inhalation. The cerebrum, or cerebral cortex, is the control center for this voluntary action.

Correct Breathing for
Effective Voice Production

Because breath vibrated in the larynx is the basis for voice production, incorrect breathing habits or inadequate breath control can be partially responsible for almost all voice quality defects. It is important in your voice-improvement program that you check very carefully for correct respiration. The process itself is a complicated one, with places for many pitfalls. There are three types of breathing patterns: the clavicular, the thoracic, and the thoracic-abdominal (or central breathing). Because we believe that the thoracic-abdominal method is best suited to speech needs, it will be discussed first.

The torso of the body is divided into two cavities: (1) the thoracic cavity, which extends from the clavicles to the waistline, and (2) the abdominal cavity, which extends from the waist to the pelvic area. These two cavities are separated at the midriff by the diaphragm, a dome-shaped muscle that is attached to the edges of the lower ribs so that in a relaxed position it looks like an open umbrella, opening upward toward the thoracic area and forming the floor of this cavity. The thorax, or chest, is composed of the rib cage, which is made up of the sternum (breast bone), twelve pairs of ribs, and the spinal column. The lungs are housed in this cavity. All of the ribs are attached to the backbone, but the attachments in the front vary, thus forming a structure capable of considerable movement. The last two pairs of ribs are floating ribs, the next four pairs are attached to each other by cartilage, and the upper six pairs of ribs are joined to the sternum. This arrangement of the musculature makes possible two movements of the thoracic cavity that are important in inhalation—an upward and forward movement and a back-to-front expansion. A third action is an elongation of this cavity due to the downward movement of the diaphragm.

Your own individual respiration process was initiated at the birth cry, and this life process is concerned with an involuntary rhythmic pattern of contraction and relaxation of the thorax. Because of this contracting and relaxing movement a partial vacuum is created in the thoracic cavity in the lung area, resulting in an imbalance of air pressure between that inside the cavity and that outside the body. This has to be rectified for survival, so nature allows air to rush in through the nasal and oral cavities, serving two purposes: (1) that of oxidation of the bloodstream, and (2) that of equalizing the air pressure. The air enters the oral and nasal cavities, passes through the trachea (windpipe), enters the bronchial tubes, the bronchioles, and fills the alveoli, or air sacs, which comprise the lungs. The lungs themselves do not move, but the expansion action of the rib cage allows room for the air sacs of the lungs to fill with air. As this action takes place we have the concomitant contraction of the diaphragm, forcing this muscle into a flattened position and thereby elongating the thoracic cavity. The diaphragm is a very important muscle in respiration because its involuntary action in inhalation necessarily involves the action of the muscles of the abdominal cavity for effective breath control. As the diaphragm contracts, the viscera (soft organs) are pushed gently downward, causing the abdominal wall to protrude slightly. Immediately the opposite muscular action takes place, and exhalation begins. The abdominal muscles contract, pushing the viscera upward as the diaphragm assumes an "open umbrella" position. This action of the diaphragm allows the muscles of the rib cage to return to their relaxed position. Meanwhile, the air is forced out of the lungs and passes through the trachea and between the vocal folds.

Now you are ready to check your own respiration habits.

1.   Lie on a flat surface, preferably the floor, place a light book or magazine on the abdominal cavity and *relax*. Do not think about your breathing pattern; just close your eyes and do nothing. After a few minutes, take note of the gentle rising and falling motion of the book. Apply your knowledge of the previous paragraphs. You should recall that during quiet breathing, the inhalation phase involves the upward and forward movement of the chest cavity. Conversely, during exhalation, the chest cavity relaxes and so does the abdominal cavity. This is effective central breathing for life.

2.   Now stand up. Check your posture. See that you are as relaxed as you were in the position on the floor. Keep the shoulders comfortably high, and do not hump over at the waist, because this interferes with the effective functioning of the diaphragm. Straighten your knees. Place your hands on your chest and breathe quietly. Does this cavity function with a rising and falling motion? It should do so. Now place your hands over the abdominal wall, with light pressure of the fingertips on the broad bands of muscle that make up the front wall of the abdomen. Again breathe quietly. Is there a protrusion of this area in inhalation? Is there a relaxing motion on exhalation? If you are breathing efficiently with the use of the thoracic and abdominal muscles, you should have a distinct upward-and-out movement of these two cavities.

You may now be aware that you do not habitually breathe in this manner. If this is so, then the second skill that you must acquire in your voice-improvement program is effective central breathing.

Some further information may be helpful in understanding respiration. In breathing for speech, central breathing is considered the most efficient, because it uses the gross abdominal muscles in exhalation. These muscles are most effective in controlling the outgoing air stream so that it can be emitted smoothly and evenly. This kind of breath emission is necessary for a firm, well-produced voice. The breath must not be allowed to "gush out." Neither must tension be allowed to develop in the thoracic cavity by pushing on the thoracic muscles in exhalation, and most important, no hypertension must develop in the pharyngeal area in an effort to emit the breath. The breath must be controlled by a strong, steady push by the gross abdominal muscles. This technique is known as *support of tone*. Specifically, this skill involves the use of the muscles of the abdominal cavity to exert a controlled muscular pressure in order to support a steady stream of breath between the vocal folds.

Try the following to help you recognize the various types of muscular action that can be present in exhalation.

1. Place one hand on each side of the chest area, with fingertips almost touching at the line of the sternum. Inhale a large amount of air, and then gently push with your hands on the chest cavity as you exhale. Feel the muscular action in this area as the air is expelled from the lungs. You should feel a "collapsing" of the muscles.

2. Now place one hand on each side of the midriff, with fingertips meeting at the front. (You are now directly over the diaphragm.) Inhale again, but this time deliberately push in on the muscles in this area as you exhale. You are now using the diaphragmatic muscles in exhalation.

3. Effective central breathing demands even more muscular control than the above exercises. You are now ready to feel the action of the gross abdominal muscles in effective exhalation. Place one hand on each side of the abdominal cavity, fingertips almost touching. (This is the location of the viscera—soft organs.) You recall from your reading in this chapter that on the phase of inhalation, the muscles in this area expand. So, as you breathe, this time on exhalation concentrate on pushing in on the gross abdominal muscles. Feel a "collapsing" of these muscles as you release the breath stream out of the oral cavity. This is giving your breath muscular "support." With this kind

of muscular action, as the vocal folds vibrate, the breath will
be released in a steady, firm stream. The end result should be
a strong, firm basic laryngeal tone.

If in speaking the occasion demands a lot of breath for a
lengthy sentence or a strong breath to express a vivid emotion,
the "extra" breath need not come from more breath being taken
in on inhalation but rather should be the result of control in emission of breath in exhalation. If you feel that you must take in
more breath on inhalation, remember that it is not acquired by
gasping with an *inward* movement or a pulling *in* of the abdominal cavity as you inhale. A clavicular breather is often
guilty of this kind of incorrect muscular action.

In clavicular breathing, the clavicles (collarbones) are used to
help raise the thoracic cavity on inhalation, so that instead of
the *correct expansion* action there is a limited *lifting* action of this
cavity. The result is unsatisfactory, because the lungs can be
only partially filled with air. Hypertension in the thoracic muscles
limits the expansion of this cavity, thereby limiting the amount
of air to be inhaled. More serious is the effect inhalation has on
the larynx. In an effort to raise the thorax by using the clavicles,
the muscles in the pharynx, surrounding the larynx, are also
placed under strain. This results in hypertension in the laryngeal
muscles, and the voice quality is directly affected. Usually the
quality is *breathy, thin,* and sometimes *strident,* the latter depending on the amount of resonator hypertension. The pitch of the
voice is necessarily adversely affected. On exhalation, clavicular
breathing is also undependable. Because there is a shallow intake
of breath, the speaker either has to rely on added strain in the
thoracic or pharyngeal areas to sustain the voice or he must
resort to quick intakes of air as he phonates. This gasping for
breath is distracting to his listeners and certainly interferes with
meaningful phrasing in his speaking.

Before we analyze and discuss the faulty voice qualities resulting from inadequate respiration, we will give suggestions for
developing effective central breathing. Practice the following
exercises, making use of all possible sensory help—the visual,
tactile, kinesthetic, and aural. Effective respiration is basic to
your voice-improvement program.

Exercises for Developing
Central Breathing

In the following exercises keep in mind and try to develop:

1. Good posture.
2. Self-awareness of adequate muscle tonus and an avoidance of hypertension in the pharyngeal area.
3. A steady, even flow of breath on exhalation.

Exercises

1. Standing with feet firmly on the floor, knees straight, hands placed over the abdominal cavity, take a deep breath. Count from one to six as you exhale. Begin the count at the *peak of inhalation*—do not allow any breath to escape before you say the number one. Concentrate on expelling all of your breath by the time you reach the last number. Do this exercise on one intake of breath. During this practice, take note of the movement of the gross abdominal muscles. There should be a gentle muscular action *inward* as you exhale.

2. Repeat the above exercise, trying for different ranges of breath control.
   a. Count from one to twelve.
   b. Count from one to six.
   c. Count from one to ten, and so on.

   This exercise is designed to make you aware tactually and kinesthetically of the fact that *you* are in control of your breath emission as you speak. At this stage of voice improvement, do not let the phase of exhalation *just happen*. Be deliberate in your control.

3. The following paragraph is composed of sentences that grow progressively longer in length. Using the same approach as in Exercises 1 and 2, read the sentences in the paragraph with an intake of breath on the first word of the sentence and plan complete exhalation at the period. You might find that the amount of intake of air will have to be varied slightly as the sentence becomes longer in length. However, the important technique will be to control the emission of breath.

Begin now. Notice your posture. Stand with straight knees.
During practice aim for central breathing. Do you know the
meaning of this? Inhale with an open, relaxed oral cavity and
unclenched back teeth. Begin to speak at the peak of inhalation
with no escape of air before you phonate. During exhalation,
attempt to control the breath stream so that you will have
enough breath to complete the sentences. It is important that
you feel a push from your gross abdominal muscles as you try
to control the outgoing breath stream. This muscular control is
important in effective voice production because this control
will help you to maintain a firm, steady stream of breath during
phonation.

Voice Qualities Affected by
Inadequate Respiration Habits

The *thin* voice is the result of poor resonance, but basic to its
misproduction is inadequate respiration. This kind of voice almost always has as its foundation clavicular breathing. The inhalation phase is shallow, and the speaker is constantly striving
for enough breath to complete his sentences. The term for this
latter defect is *voice fading*. Because the speaker makes no use
of the abdominal muscles, he must constantly take in more breath
(for each phrase), resorting to quick intakes of air in order to
complete his formulated thoughts. This is why the person with a
thin voice usually has a slightly breathy quality. He takes in
quick gasps of air, does not resonate it effectively, and then lets
it spill out of the oral cavity without having used it construc-
tively during phonation.

The *breathy* voice also involves poor respiration habits. The
basic defects in this voice quality are failure to attain adduction
(closing) of the vocal folds during phonation (this will be discussed fully in Chapter 7), failure to use the gross abdominal
muscles to control a steady stream of released breath, and finally,
a faulty respiration pattern. In many cases, the speaker's breathing habits are not of the clavicular type, but most such speakers
use only slight diaphragmatic action and are not at all aware of
the use of the abdominal muscles for support of vocal tone.

The three defective qualities of *stridency*, *harshness*, and *hoarseness* are the direct result of hypertension—the *strident* voice having hypertension in the resonators, the *harsh* and *hoarse* voices having hypertension within the laryngeal area. However, all three conditions can or may suffer from the lack of effective breath control. Increased breath pressure beneath the vocal folds is needed for the projection of your voice. In order to accumulate this breath pressure and in order to sustain it, there must be increased use of the gross abdominal muscles for the necessary "energy" needed. If the speaker is not aware of the use of the abdominal muscles to increase the projection of his voice, he quite naturally increases the tension of the muscles in the pharyngeal and laryngeal areas. The result can be stridency, harshness, or hoarseness, depending on accompanying conditions. So here we face the situation of a speaker possibly having taken in enough air on inhalation, but in his attempt to build energy for increased projection, foregoes adequate support of tone and uses incorrect muscular action on exhalation. He should have used the gross abdominal muscles to push out a strong, steady stream of breath. Instead, he incorrectly uses the muscles of the larynx in attempting to build up needed pressure for projection. A specific example of this kind of incorrect projection is the *hoarse* voice. The term *hoarseness* is usually used to describe the voice that has suffered from vocal abuse. The sports event where you have screamed energetically and enthusiastically, the social affair where you have talked above the dance band all evening—these kinds of events provide conditions for vocal abuse. Hoarseness can be a temporary condition, as seen from the examples just cited, or it can be a chronic condition. You can have a postnasal drip or a sinus irritation, which would irritate the membraneous tissues of the throat. The use of constantly inflamed tissues could result in a chronic hoarseness. Obviously a medical doctor should be consulted before any vocal therapy is attempted.

Now that you have begun work in two areas of voice improvement, this is a good time to clarify the use of material in your practice sessions. In your work the kind of printed material you use is not important (not so in articulation, where material containing the exact sounds you wish to improve should be used),

but in voice practice *what you do with the material is important.*
For example, if you are trying to acquire effective oral resonance
coupled with central breathing, a paragraph of words is of no
more benefit than saying the alphabet or counting numbers. In
fact, reading material from a book can be distracting to your concentration. Rather, in the initial stages of voice work, use the
alphabet, use numbers, and then as you gain confidence, try saying phrases that you use in daily conversation. Here is a partial
list.

Hello!	(*Watch excessive push of breath on the / h /.*)
Good morning.	(*A challenge for those with assimilation nasality.*)
How are you?	(*Watch / h / sound.*)
I'm fine.	(*Note use of velum on non-nasal sounds.*)
What are we having for breakfast?	(*A good combination of voiced and voiceless sounds for those with breathy voices.*)

Where is your next class?
Let's shop at the market on Thursday this week.
The chairman is calling a committee meeting for tomorrow at nine
A.M. Can you attend? And so on.

The following breath control exercise can be helpful to most
types of voice problems. The object of this exercise is to encourage
a free-flowing emission of breath out of the pharyngeal cavity
into the oral cavity and *out of the mouth.* The *strident* voice, the
thin voice, and the *throaty* voice usually leave the breath back
"in the throat" instead of pushing the outgoing breath stream
toward the front of the mouth. This kind of breath control emission can be done more successfully if there is an open oral cavity,
a relaxed pharyngeal cavity, and a firm, steady breath stream.

Hold the palm of your hand about four inches away from your
mouth. Place your other hand over the abdominal cavity. Count from
one to ten, taking a breath for the individual numbers. On each count
gently push the air stream out of the oral cavity and against the palm
of your hand. There will be, of course, more breath emission on some
numbers than on others because of the nature of the sounds produced
(Plosives will have more breath emission than nasals). As you are

doing this exercise, attempt to feel muscular action in the abdominal cavity. If the voice begins to sound too breathy, try for more oral resonance by allowing the breath (sounds) to resonate a little longer in the oral cavity. Work for a "round" feeling in the mouth. Keep in mind a relaxed pharyngeal cavity and put the tension on the gross abdominal muscles.

Exercises

Use any of the suggestions and exercises in this chapter, but note the individual approach for the particular voice problem as stated below.

For the strident voice (termed *raspy* if the pitch is too low):

1. Relaxed resonators—oral and pharyngeal.
2. Open oral cavity—open back teeth.
3. Effective central breathing.

For the thin voice—voice fading:

1. Relaxed pharyngeal and oral cavities.
2. Open oral cavity.
3. Correct central breathing.
4. Greater use of abdominal muscles to attain a strong, steady stream of breath for phonation.
5. For voice fading—keep the stream of breath going until the *end of the sentence.* Do not allow the breath support to diminish as you reach the end of the sentence. Attempt to say the final syllables in the sentence as loudly as you said the first syllables.

For the throaty voice:

1. Relaxed oral cavity.
2. A flexible tongue—very important.
3. A decided effort to get the voice "up and out" of your throat. Stand about six feet away from a wall. Keep your chin level, but raise your eyes slightly upward, and aim to

send the voice to a chosen spot on the wall. Get the feeling of "bouncing" your voice against the wall. Use the gross abdominal muscles.

For the harsh voice:

1. Use the same exercises as those for the throaty voice. The main problems of the harsh voice are hyperpharyngeal and hyperlaryngeal tension and a failure to get the voice out of the throat.

CHAPTER 7

Laryngeal Tension

BECAUSE voice is the product of exhaled breath vibrated at the vocal folds, then the control and manipulation of the larynx can be a vital factor in avoiding defective voice qualities. Since you must be able to control the larynx for effective phonation and since you might have to learn how to manipulate the larynx to improve any faulty voice production, let us take a close look at the anatomy and physiology of this organ of speech.

Anatomy and Physiology of the Larynx

The larynx, or "voice box," rests on top of the trachea (windpipe) to form a continuous tube that opens into the pharynx. This is commonly known as the laryngopharynx area. The larynx is made up of nine cartilages bound together by ligaments and membranous tissue. There is one bone in the larynx, the hyoid bone, from which the larynx is suspended. The hyoid bone, in turn, is suspended from the back of the tongue. This particular structure is worth mentioning because it reinforces the influencing effect of articulatory movement, specifically the movement of the tongue, on effective phonation.

For our purpose, it is relatively unimportant for you to know the names and location of all of the parts of the larynx. Only those parts of the larynx will be included that will contribute to your knowledge of the physiology of the larynx and the parts that will have a direct bearing on your manipulation of this organ.

You should become acquainted with the following parts of the larynx (*see* Figure 5-1):

1. Hyoid bone—larynx suspended from this bone.
2. Thyroid cartilage—forms the contour of the larynx; vocal folds attached to center of front, inside wall of this cartilage.
3. Cricoid cartilage—forms last section of larynx, directly attached to trachea.
4. Arytenoid cartilages—a pair of pyramid-shaped cartilages to which the vocal folds are attached at the rear of the larynx.
5. Vocal folds—vibrating body that produces basic laryngeal tone as breath is emitted between them.
6. Glottis—opening between the folds.

Biologically, the main function of the larynx is to prevent food from entering the trachea and protect the lungs. The vocal folds act also as a valve during any form of physical exertion by preventing the emission of air from out of the lungs. In speech the larynx acts as the organ of voice production. It has previously been stated in this text that the process of phonation involves the emission of breath between the vocal folds, breath which is then set into vibration by the movement of the folds, resonated in the three resonating cavities, and emitted as sounds by the movement of the articulators. In this chapter we will consider the factors that contribute to the correct functioning of the larynx and how malfunctioning of the larynx can result in defective voice quality.

The *extrinsic* muscles of the larynx aid in the positioning of the larynx. These muscles connect the larynx to the hyoid bone and to other parts of the pharynx, and they are also concerned in part with the movement of the larynx in swallowing and coughing. These muscles are of importance in voice production only if you have hypertension in the pharynx or in the musculature of the jaws, tension that affects the larynx proper. The result can be an unnaturally high-pitch level or an obvious strain in your voice quality. Place your fingertips on the larynx and then swallow. Take close note of the fact that the larynx is not a tense organ but that it does become tense—that is, *adequately tense* (muscle tonus)—when you swallow. In the same manner, you can develop adequate muscle tonus for improved voice production.

The *intrinsic* muscles of the larynx have as their main function the opening and closing of the vocal folds. These may be limited to the general categories of the *abductors,* which open the vocal folds, the *adductors,* which close the folds, the *tensors,* which stretch and elongate the folds, and the *relaxors,* which relax and shorten the folds. These muscles have their origin and insertion within the larynx itself. The opening and closing of the vocal folds is controlled by a slight rocking motion of the thyroid cartilage, by movements of the arytenoid cartilages, and by pairs of antagonistic muscles connected to and from the thyroid cartilage, the cricoid cartilage, and the arytenoids. There is nerve stimulation (innervation) by the tenth cranial nerve, the vagus nerve, and more specifically by the laryngeal branch, which stimulates the larynx itself.

The Musculature of the Larynx in the Production of Voice

Organs and Muscles	Movement	Purpose
Thyroid cartilage is connected in front to the cricoid cartilage.	Slight rocking back and forth.	Affects opening and closing of folds.
Cricoid cartilage forms posterior wall of the larynx.		
Arytenoid cartilage's base joins with cricoid cartilage, forming a joint.	Pivoting motion; gentle rocking back and forth; sliding together and apart.	Directly involved with the adduction and abduction of the vocal folds.
Adductor and abductor muscles.		Shorten, lengthen, tense, relax vocal folds.

Even though the muscles mentioned above act involuntarily in that you cannot control them individually and directly, the knowledge of the involvement of these muscles in phonation can be most helpful. You can experience kinesthetically and tactually the changes in movements of the larynx as it functions, and this awareness should further your control over the larynx. The real test of control demonstrates itself in terms of the results you get as you try to manipulate the larynx. For example, by now you know what it means to relax your lower jaw and to maintain oral activity. You know that this kind of effort releases hypertension in the laryngeal area and therefore takes some of the strain out of your voice. You should feel secure with this improvement in voice quality because you can feel (tactile) the difference in muscle tension as you spread your hand over the area. Your "muscle sense" (kinesthetic) further supports your experience, and possibly by now you can even hear (aural) the beginnings of change from strident to more mellow quality. From now until the end of this chapter you will be called upon to use all of your faculties to help you improve your voice.

The vocal folds are the vibrating body in the production of voice. During respiration for life they move back and forth slightly; during a deliberate gasp or quick intake of breath, the folds are held wide apart. In a loud whisper they are closed at the anterior portion and held apart at the posterior portion. This is important, for you might think that you are saving your voice by whispering if you are suffering from laryngitis. This is a strained position for the vocal folds. Do not whisper if you are suffering from a cold or have some other physical irritation. Rather, speak *softly* so that the folds can vibrate evenly at the mid-line. In phonation for speech this is their normal position.

It is obvious from this discussion that the movement of the vocal folds in the production of voice involves a complex muscular action. For the purposes of your voice-improvement program it is important for you to know only *how* the functioning of the larynx affects your particular voice problem. What you are specifically concerned with is *adequate muscle tonus.* Because the larynx is not basically a hypertense organ, it is your problem to see that it does not become so. By now you are well aware that the muscles of the oral cavity, of the pharynx, and of the thoracic cavity all have a bearing on increasing the tension in the larynx or in helping the larynx to maintain just enough muscle tonus to produce a good basic laryngeal tone. Muscle tonus implies a firmness—not a hypertenseness in the larynx. There must be just the right amount of *muscle firmness* to produce vocal tone.

Adequate muscle tonus in the larynx is directly related to effective respiration habits. If there is a good, firm, steady stream of breath passing between the vocal folds, then the folds are more apt to respond with a firmness rather than a laxness in muscular action. Conversely, if the breath is emitted with a sudden force *before* the folds begin to vibrate for phonation, then you will experience a *glottal attack*. This unpleasant vocal sound is particularly related to the vowel sounds produced low in the mouth and to the diphthongs. As you produce the sounds of / ɑ /, / æ /, / ɪ / and / aʊ /, try for a smooth initiation of tone. Try to avoid a sudden release of air before phonation. Release the breath smoothly and evenly. A relaxed tongue and lower jaw are helpful also.

Exercises for Developing Adequate Laryngeal Tension

1. With gently closed lips, begin a slow "chewing" motion with your jaws. Continue for about 6–8 seconds, and then gradually begin to hum—*hmmmmmmmmmmmm*. The sound that will be emitted is generally a clear, firm, fully resonated tone. A tone produced in this manner usually has *adequate muscle tonus*, and this is the kind of basic quality toward which you must strive in daily voice production.

2. This time part the lips slightly, and place the tongue tip *firmly* in position for the lingua-alveolar sound of / n /. Begin the sound, meanwhile keeping your fingertips gently placed over the larynx. Feel the vibration in this area as you say / n /. Concentrate on avoiding any accompanying / h / sound, which is air escaping between the vocal folds without being vibrated. When there is an excessive amount of this unvibrated air, there is certain to be inadequate muscle tonus in the larynx. The resultant voice quality is breathy.

3. Continue the exercises in number 2, using for variety the following *voiced continuants* in American English: / m /, / ŋ /, / v /, / z /, / ł /, / ʒ /, / j /, / w /. We encourage you

to do this exercise often if you have a breathy voice. (Five
minutes out of every available hour of the day would be suffi-
cient.) The muscles of the larynx will acquire adequate muscle
tonus only by consistent and correct exercise.

Inadequate laryngeal tension and ineffective respiration habits
can also result in nodules (nodes) on the vibrating edges of the
vocal folds. The presence of such nodules usually gives the voice
a breathy, husky quality. Let it be understood that such a quality
is not always the sign of existing nodules. (A breathy, husky
voice can be the result of ineffective voice production.) The
presence of nodules can be determined by a laryngologist (a
specialist in the study and treatment of the larynx) during a
laryngological examination, at which time the vocal mechanism
is closely examined. If nodules are present, the laryngologist de-
termines the treatment. Frequently the patient is placed on vocal
rest (silence) for a period of time in the hope that the nodules
will diminish in size or disappear. In other instances the vocal
folds are stripped and the nodules removed. In any event, if
such a condition is suspected, a laryngological examination is of
primary importance. Then vocal therapy can proceed along the
lines recommended in this handbook for the improvement of the
breathy, husky voice.

Although a study of the frequency and amplitude of sound
waves, and the relationship of these factors to pitch, are not
areas of concern here, you should know what influences the
change of pitch in your voice and how you can manipulate and
control it. The use of pitch variation in meaningful speech will be
considered in Chapter 8. In this chapter we will examine the area
of pitch as it is directly related to your control over the movements of the vocal folds. More specifically we will examine how
the general overall production of voice affects the pitch of your
voice.

At the outset, the authors would like to state clearly that they
firmly believe that voice produced correctly is generally the
answer to most "pitch" problems. The authors of this text are
firmly against changing the pitch level of a voice without serious
reason. Raising the pitch level of a low, breathy voice or of a

low, harsh voice is not the only answer. In fact, raising the pitch level could result in a high, breathy voice or a strident voice. Unless a person is a voice-improvement specialist, he should not decide to manipulate his pitch, because if this is not done with skill and technical knowledge, vocal damage can be the result.

In this text the primary thesis of voice improvement is that correct, effective, overall voice production is an intelligent approach to almost all voice problems. Effective production means dependable respiration habits, effective resonance, and adequate laryngeal tension. Voice if it is well produced, like water, will seek its own level—its own optimum-pitch level. This means that with correct production the voice will seek that pitch range at which it displays the least amount of strain and functions most efficiently. It is then the problem of the student to make this optimum pitch range his habitual pitch range.

The pitch of your voice is controlled by an increase of tension in the vocal folds and by the amount of air pressure beneath them. The amount of tension in turn influences the thickness and elasticity of the folds. All of these factors determine the highness or lowness of the pitch you are using. Consider the strings on the piano. The longer, more elastic strings produce the mellow, full notes, whereas the stretched, tense strings produce the high notes. The vocal folds function in much the same manner. If you have been told that you have a high-pitched voice, you can be almost sure that your main problem is hypertension—excessive tension in the larynx, the pharynx, or in the thoracic cavity. If you have been advised that your pitch is too low, you could be doing a number of things incorrectly. Perhaps you are not "firming up" the laryngeal muscles enough, or perhaps you are pushing the voice down into the pharynx and not allowing it to come out of the throat and be resonated in the oral cavity.

Breath pressure beneath the vocal folds can also vary the pitch. If you are trying to develop increased volume in your voice (this will be discussed further in Chapter 8), you must use more "energy" and increase the intensity of the pressure of air under the folds. This increased intensity will result in increased volume of voice. You should have become aware of this fact as you did the exercises in respiration skills in Chapter 6. However, your pitch must not rise in the process. In other words, you must not tense the vocal folds in order to increase the intensity but rather use the gross abdominal muscles for increased air pressure. This kind of voice production is necessary for a pleasant voice quality coupled with increased volume. Hyperlaryngeal tension only raises the pitch and adds a strident quality to the voice.

In the chapter on respiration (Chapter 6) *voice fading* was mentioned. This ineffective use of voice has as its basis poor respiration habits and lack of support of tone (inadequate use of gross abdominal muscles). As this kind of voice is projected, there is usually the accompanying factor of hyperlaryngeal tension which causes the pitch to rise. If you are unable to project your voice enough to be heard or if you are frequently asked to repeat the ends of your sentences, then voice fading is probably your problem. First check yourself for central breathing (do the exercises in Chapter 6, page 143), and then consider the following suggestions:

1. Concentrate on balance of resonance, adequate laryngeal tension, and most important, support of tone by using your gross abdominal muscles. For the last skill try the following exercises.

   Using numbers ranging from one to ten, say each number with conversational volume, and immediately repeat the number with projected voice. Place your hand over the abdominal muscles and *feel* the push on these muscles as you use them to increase the volume on the louder number. *Do not change* your pitch of voice. There should be no hypertension in the larynx.

   one (conversational tone); one (projected tone); two (conversational tone); two (projected tone); etc.

2. Using the numbers from one to ten again, say them all on *one* intake of breath, and try to say the final numbers (eight–nine–ten) with the same amount of volume as the first numbers (one–two–three). Keep the voice going by pushing on the abdominal muscles to sustain the breath until the number ten. If the breath gives out, you are probably not controlling your exhalation properly.

Faulty Voice Qualities Involved with Hyperlaryngeal and Hypolaryngeal Tension

Quality	Problems	Corrective Procedures
Strident voice	Some hypertension in laryngeal area due to hypertension in laryngopharynx and oropharynx; faulty respiration habits.	Relax pharyngeal and oral resonating cavities; support tone with gross abdominal muscles.
Thin voice	Hypertension in the larynx resulting in high-pitch range; poor balance of resonance; slight breathiness.	Relax laryngeal muscles; increase oral resonance; support tone with gross abdominal muscles.
Breathy voice	Hypotension of the vocal folds; shallow breathing.	Firm up laryngeal muscles; develop gross abdominal muscle control.
Husky voice	Hypotension of the vocal folds; shallow breathing; narrow pitch range (low).	Firm up laryngeal muscles; develop gross abdominal muscle control; project voice up and out of throat.
Harsh voice	Hypertension in extrinsic laryngeal muscles; hypertension in laryngeal muscles; overenergizing and overprojection.	Relax pharyngeal area; develop oral resonance; control volume.
Hoarse voice	Possible physiological condition; hypertension in vocal folds accompanied by excessive push of breath at glottis.	Treatment of medical problem; develop relaxed pharyngeal area; work on smooth initiation of tone.
Glottal attacks	Hypertension in the vocal folds (hypertension before tone is initiated) and folds exploded open.	Relax the laryngeal muscles by working on smooth initiation of tone; use gross abdominal muscular action.

CHAPTER 8

Vocal Skills
in Speaking

A WELL-PRODUCED voice along with correct, assimilated sounds is a good beginning for an effective communication pattern. The following pages in this chapter will concentrate on helping you to improve your communication skills in three areas: meaningful pitch variation, adequate volume, and controlled rate.

The mental twister "Which is more important, what is said or how it is said?" can have some significance in this chapter. The authors firmly believe that what is said is of paramount importance (in terms of content of message, of the reasoning and evidence employed, and of the personal, psychological, and ethical elements included), but the authors likewise believe that what is said can be more effective in its impact *if it is said more meaningfully.*

You have already concentrated on the correction of faulty diction, and you have learned not only how to make sounds correctly but how to avoid possible deviations in the sounds articulated. While acquiring these skills, you were improving at the same time the oral and nasal resonance in your voice. By working on oral activity (opening the oral cavity, unclenching the back teeth, and maintaining a relaxed lower jaw) and working on articulatory movement (using the articulators correctly and with precision), you found that you were well on the way to a more resonant voice. That is why we began with resonance in the opening chapter of Part II, reminded you of the importance of this newly acquired skill, and then asked you to concentrate on a balance of resonance in your voice by including effective pharyngeal resonance. We concentrated next on respiration, trying to acquire support of tone by learning how to use the gross abdominal muscles in exhalation. Finally you became aware of the functioning of the vocal folds and the need for adequate laryngeal tension. It was at this point that you encouraged changes in pitch and, to some extent, changes in volume. You have already learned some basic theories concerning pitch variation, which you should review:

1. The vocal folds are the vibrating body of voice production.
2. Exhaled breath passes between the vocal folds and is set into vibration and forms sound waves.
3. The sound waves have differences in frequency and in wave length.
4. These differences are known as the differences in pitch.

Pitch Variation

Changes in the pitch of your voice depend on many factors, some simple, others very complex. Physiologically, pitch is governed by the tension, length, and thickness of the vocal folds. Directly influencing the functioning of the vocal folds are numerous other factors. As you may have noticed, your *physical state* contributes to the pitch changes in your voice. Following an illness, when respiration control is minimal, your voice is apt to sound thin, breathy, and weak. Also, the pitch is frequently higher, because in your effort to project your voice (you realize that you sound "weak"), you tense the vocal folds. (At this point you might review the relationship of tension and thinness of the vocal folds to increased vibration, the direct result of which is raised pitch—Chapter 7.) Your *mental state*, or attitude, also has a decided effect on the changes of pitch in your voice. In anger, pitch changes in voice are various, depending on the individual. Some people express their anger under such tension that the voice is high-pitched and strained. Others in anger tense the pharyngeal cavity while keeping their voices concentrated in that area so that the voice is low-pitched and harsh, and many sound as if the person is "talking through his teeth" or "biting off his words." The last factor that influences pitch levels is faulty voice production. Review Chapter 5 for this explanation.

Before turning your attention to meaningful pitch variation, you should become acquainted with the methods used to vary your pitch consciously. Place your fingertips on the larynx and swallow. You will feel the slight tension in the laryngeal muscles as the larynx moves. Open your mouth comfortably wide, and hold it open as you move the back part of your tongue. Feel the pull on the larynx. Both of these experiences should show you that you are manipulating the extrinsic muscles of the larynx. In order to change the pitch of your voice, the intrinsic muscles of the larynx must be manipulated so that the folds will change their length, thickness, and tension. Before you can vary your pitch meaningfully, you need to assure yourself that you are able to vary the pitch—that your voice can assume different tones of sound. Experiment with the following suggestions:

Use the alphabet so that your vocal tone will not be influenced by word meaning. Say each letter on a different pitch. What pitch you use is unimportant. Say one letter high, the next lower, the next letter higher than the first, and so on. The main point is to *deliberately* control the pitch of your voice. *Listen* carefully for changes in tone. Are you able to *aurally* detect the differences in voice? If not, continue to do this exercise until your ear begins to discriminate. You might benefit from using the piano keyboard as a guide. Say the letters of the alphabet on the different keys—changing notes indiscriminately. A word of caution: as you do this exercise keep in mind open oral cavity and relaxed jaws in order to avoid hyperlaryngeal tension. Attempt to say the higher tones and lower tones with similar balanced resonance as on the notes in the middle of your range.

In Chapter 6, "Respiration," you were reminded that respiration habits had a specific effect on the functioning of the laryngeal muscles. If the breath is exhaled steadily and smoothly, the voice quality is pleasant, and this is controlled, of course, by a steady pressure on the abdominal muscles during exhalation. If the pressure is allowed to originate in the laryngeal area, then the pressure will cause tension in the vocal folds (hyperlaryngeal tension) and hence cause the pitch to rise as you speak.

Review the practice material in Chapter 7, page 156.

Pitch is affected by your own personality and temperament. To a large extent the meaning of the words you articulate is conveyed very specifically by variations in pitch. For effective use of voice, it is helpful if you have a wide pitch range. Your voice is capable of a least an octave range, and some trained voices can use a range of one and a half octaves. Do not limit your use of voice by concentrating on one section of your potential range. Frequently students will use only the high-pitch range or the low-pitch range of their voices as they speak, and when this is called to their attention, their immediate reaction is usually, "But, I don't want to lower (or raise) my pitch." This is not the problem. An effective pitch range will allow you to *keep* the range you are using, but it will also allow you to *extend* it to include the range you are not using. If you only raise a low-pitched voice, the result is just another pitch problem—a high-pitched voice. Only to lower a high voice to a narrow low range is equally undesirable.

The term *melody* is used to indicate your own individual pitch changes as you speak. Your pitch variations are made up of inflections—a rising inflection ⟋ , a falling inflection ⟍ , and the circumflex inflection ⟋⟍ , which is a combination within a word or a phrase of the rising and falling inflections. The melody pattern of your voice is necessarily influenced by how you feel about what you are saying. Because your muscles react in response to your emotional feelings, your voice is necessarily affected in the same manner. The muscles involved in the expression of your ideas are affected in their movements not only by your feelings about your ideas but by the ideas themselves. There is a third component. Your voice may also be affected by your *reactions* to your feelings about your ideas. Perhaps you have some thoughts on the administrative policies of your school or office. You may have some pretty strong negative reactions to present policies, but at the same time you are upset because you have them. You are plagued by the idea that having these negative reactions might indicate a lack of loyalty on your part to the school or office, so that when you comment on the administrative policies you find yourself highly emotionally charged. These reaction feelings probably demonstrate themselves in a loudly projected voice, one whose quality is perhaps strident or raspy and high-pitched.

Whatever the hypothetical or real situation, it is far better to let the emotions display themselves through your voice. If you are able to demonstrate anger, irritation, or impatience, so by the same token your voice will be capable of showing warmth, sincerity, and tolerance. The voice that is monotonous is sometimes the real problem. This voice has minimal pitch variation and certainly has less "voice color." This type of voice is erroneously called a monotone by some people. Physiologically speaking, to sustain a *monotone* in your pitch is impossible. Due to the complex nature of the various movements of the vocal folds, the muscles controlling these movements are incapable of maintaining the rigid positioning needed to sustain "one tone" of voice. Rather, this voice tends to use the same pattern of pitch variations within a very limited range to express a variety of ideas.

Although techniques of public speaking and oral reading are outside the province of this handbook, we feel that it is important to consider one other technique involved in effective use of voice that could specifically contribute to your becoming a polished speaker or a vivid oral reader. The term *vocal color* is nebulous, but the result of the skill involved is most concrete. Simply stated, this skill involves letting your voice take on the meaning and mood of the words you are saying. For example, consider the two following phrases:

Isn't it a lovely day!
I feel very fatigued.

The wording of the two individual sentences strongly suggests a different meaning and particularly a different mood. The first sentence ("Isn't it a lovely day!") suggests a brightness of tonal quality, a "light" voice, as in contrast with the second sentence ("I feel very fatigued"), which suggests a heavy mood, one lacking in spirit and energy. In order to communicate effectively the meaning of the two sentences, there should be a marked differ-ence in use of voice. The techniques involved in vocal color en-compass all the skills discussed so far in this chapter along with a deliberate attempt to let your voice *sound* like the words you are saying. Vocal color can be acquired:

1. If the voice is correctly produced so that no muscular strain is present.

2. If the respiration habits are good, because breath control is needed to express your ideas effectively. (Gasping for a quick intake of breath can interrupt the production of voice.)

3. If there is adequate amplification and modification of the laryn-geal tone. Voices with limited resonance cannot easily become flexible in "voice color."

4. If there is effective pitch variation.

5. If there is present a willingness on your part to express the emo-tional content of your words.

Point number 5 is not an easy task for some people. Physically, many of you do not react with energy and vigor because of your basic body structure. Psychologically, many of you do not react expressively because of numerous factors: home environment, early training, present apathy, lack of sensitivity, and even a dis-like for open expression of emotion. Your home environment and early training could have been one where you were subtly re-strained against showing strong emotional reactions. One home we know of stressed the need for the members of the family to express "goodness." The children were cautioned against demon-strating displeasure or anger. The entire approach to life in that home was "Think good." To think positively about life is cer-tainly commendable and even helpful, but to be noncommital even about "righteous anger" is unrealistic. Your present apathy toward life could be another contributing factor to your lack of expressiveness in voice. If you do not have some definite feelings about your present existence or future goals, then this lack of reaction can demonstrate itself in your voice. We do not mean to suggest that everyone become a dynamo in order to develop vocal color, but to react emotionally to what is happening to you and around you can stimulate spontaneous "color" in your voice. This means to say that you should *attempt* to react with some kind of interest and feeling, so that your voice in turn reacts as you speak. There are two basic approaches to this skill: (1) having control over a flexible vocal mechanism and (2) having a real understanding of what you are saying and/or having a sincere acceptance of the content of what you are saying.

Exercises for Acquiring Variation in Pitch and Vocal Color

1. Review the exercises in this chapter on page 160 for a mechanical approach to pitch variation.

2. Try the following sentences, keeping in mind the *meaning* of the words and the *mood* created by the meaning of the words.

   a. *Hello!* (Call out cheerfully to a friend across the room. Concentrate on correct projection and attempt a rising inflection.)

   b. *How are you feeling today?* (Express *concern.* Try a circumflex pitch pattern.)

   c. *Don't you dare make such an accusation!* (Express quiet anger. Intentionally try a precise diction with a monotonous tone of voice in all of the words except *dare.* On this word use a rising inflection.)

   d. Consider the word *Goodbye.* Say it with the following meanings: leaving a party of friends; parting in anger; leaving a child with whom you've been playing; anticipating a long departure from a friend.

Adequate Volume

Loudness or volume in voice production refers to the amount of audibility of the tone produced. The audibility of your voice is physically controlled at the vocal folds. As you exhale breath, pressure builds beneath the vocal folds. This pressure is one factor in initiating the vibration of the folds. Physically, you increase loudness by increasing this breath pressure at the glottis, which in turn increases the amplitude of vibration of the vocal folds. The pressure itself is built up as you use more "energy" in voice production, being careful to use the gross abdominal muscles to apply the necessary push as you exhale the breath. It is essential to keep in mind that the energy for this increase of pressure beneath the folds should not come from the thoracic cavity. If the thoracic muscles are used, tension will inevitably be extended into the pharyngeal area. This pharyngeal tension will affect the efficient functioning of the larynx, and the result will be an unpleasant, loud voice. Increased volume is inaccurately related to a raised pitch by some who do not produce voice correctly. Volume can increase as the pitch of the voice is raised for the expression of certain emotions, but to increase volume per se the pitch should not be raised. Decrease of volume takes place with the lessening of pressure beneath the vocal folds. If you wish to use less volume as you speak, you must guard against allowing the breath to escape as unphonated air, thus creating a breathy quality. This is faulty voice production and can cause vocal fatigue. A voice produced with less volume should still be a clear, firm voice, having a steady stream of breath that is being gently vibrated between the vocal folds. You should try to maintain adequate laryngeal muscle tonus even though pressure is lessened beneath the folds.

A related factor not to be discounted in trying to control the habitual loudness or softness of a person's voice is his personality. Because of the basic temperament of an individual, it might be difficult for him to increase his volume, particularly if he has acquired a thin, breathy, monotonous voice. Sometimes the problem is simply physical, with the person having to learn to use his gross abdominal muscles to get projection. In other instances, the particular type of voice production is so involved with the person as a distinct personality that trying to get him to improve his projection might require that he take a closer look at himself —a complete reappraisal of his values. Why does he speak softly? Why does he not want to speak louder? Is he basically *afraid* to

have his ideas heard? Did he come from an environment where
to speak up and be heard was disapproved? Conversely, the voice
of the person who over-projects continuously poses a problem.
This person seemingly talks at top volume even if he is speaking "confidentially" to you. He constantly overenergizes as he
pushes out the breath with great force and with much staccato.
Why does he *have* to be heard? Why must he dominate the conversation? Is his voice the product of an environment in which
one had to scream to be heard? If so, has he allowed this increased volume to transfer to his daily life, even though other
elements are no longer a threat? If you discover that you over-
energize or underproject, you may have to examine such questions before dealing with the problem.

In order to acquire effective volume control in the everyday
use of your voice keep the following in mind:

1. Check your method of increasing your volume. Be sure you
   use the gross abdominal muscles to initiate the necessary
   "energy."

2. Do not allow the increased volume to raise your pitch range
   (except if you want to do so for some emotional interpretation).

3. Do not feel that your voice must be loud at all times. Work for
   two skills—flexibility and adaptability in volume control.
   Flexibility: Let your control of volume include loud and
                  soft voice projection.

   Adaptability: Make these adjustments relate to *what* you are
                 saying. Further adaptability is related to the
                 size of the room, number of people present, and
                 so on.

Skill in the correct method of projection and skill in volume
control can be of paramount importance to you either in your
vocation or in your avocation. To be able to effectively project
the voice so that there is no vocal strain can be a real asset to
the professional person (teacher, lecturer), the businessman, or
the actor. In any public-speaking situation, whether it be a formal
speaking situation (giving a speech, lecturing to an audience,

reading the minutes at the meeting of an organization), or a teaching situation (in the classroom, a demonstration speech on a given product), or on the stage (as an actor or as an oral reader), you must be heard. If your audience cannot hear you, then your efforts in the effective delivery of good content is negligible.

Rate Control

The term *rate* refers to the number of words you speak per minute. Studies have shown that the so-called normal conversational rate is anywhere from 120–140 words per minute. Your rate when reading aloud is slightly faster, with an average between 150–180 words per minute. The term *duration* lends more information to an analysis of rate in speech. Time given to the production of sounds within a word and time given to the pauses between words are examples of duration. Your *rate* of speaking, coupled with your own pattern of *duration,* forms the basis for your individual rate profile.

Skill in rate, like skill in pitch variation and volume control, can be acquired, and you can learn to use the techniques meaningfully. Some authorities in the field of speech consider rate a comparatively easy area to master, but we tend not to agree with this idea. Those of you who have any problems with rate are well aware of the seemingly intangible complexities involved in this characteristic of speech.

There are three influences we must consider as we attempt an analysis and evaluation of rate in the speech of the individual —the physical, the intellectual, and the psychological. In the light of the importance of these influences we will consider rate of speech which is *too fast,* rate of speech which is *too slow,* rate which lacks *meaningful variety,* and rate of speech which is seemingly *adequate.*

In this handbook we have noted frequently that the differences in your own anatomy and physiology as compared with that of other people, make your problems in speech highly individual. Your rate of speech is similarly affected by your whole body structure and how your structure functions. Your native ability in physical skills and your ability to acquire more and/or finer skills is part of your physical makeup. Some of you move more quickly than others, some of you have better muscular coordination, others move quickly even though coordination is limited. Physically, your rate of speech is affected by such factors. For example, a fast rate of speaking is found most frequently in the energetic, quick-moving person. The unusual case is to find the mild-mannered, taciturn speaker with excessive rate problems. Your physical rate of speaking seems to blend in with your tempo of living, your pace in thinking, and your general overall physical movements. We wish to make the point strongly here that none of this analysis has the element of "right or wrong." Rather, the point of showing these possible relationships is to substantiate, in part, why rate problems are difficult to change.

Heredity, early environmental stimulation, conditioning, and even the type of education to which you were exposed—all these factors helped to develop your intellectual powers and also played a substantial role in affecting your pace of thinking. Have you ever played the game of *charades* and experienced the inability to decipher the cues (which are usually given at a rapid-fire pace) in time to give an answer? Still more frustrating, did you have the experience of understanding the cues given and yet not being able to formulate the answer in time or perhaps being unable to give the answer as quickly as the person next to you simply because he spoke faster than you? Obviously, the trick to playing charades successfully is not limited to IQ.

Everyone has a physical pace at which he moves comfortably and everyone has an intellectual pace at which he moves comfortably or uncomfortably. (It is irritating not to be able to give in time an answer which one knows.) In just such a way everyone has an individual emotional pace inextricably interwoven with the physical and intellectual. His rate of emotional reaction also affects his rate of speaking. He may be capable of feeling as deeply as his friend, but due to the complexities of his nature, he may not be inclined to demonstrate the emotion as quickly— either visibly or verbally.

When is rate too fast? When is rate too slow? We say your rate is too fast (1) when your speed of speaking interferes with intelligibility, and/or (2) when your speed interferes with meaningful expression so that the reaction of your listener to your content is minimized. We say your rate is too slow when your content suffers because of dullness of pace. Most of you know the acquaintance or friend who takes forever to express a few ideas.

Skill in the use of rate involves intelligibility and variation.* Give yourself *time* to say the sounds correctly and distinctly so that you will be understood. *Vary* your rate according to the *meaning* of your content. Some ideas should be expressed quickly —for example, a warning: "Watch out!"—and conversely, some ideas can be expressed slowly: "This is a sad situation." The determinant should be the meaning of the words you are saying.

Page References for Voice Improvement in Improving Voice and Articulation

Quality	Analysis	References
The strident voice	Hypertension in resonators	Chapter 5, p. 128
	Poor respiration habits	Chapter 6, p. 140
	Possible nasality	Chapter 5, p. 134
	Limited pitch range (high)	Chapter 8, p. 160
The raspy voice	Same as above except—	
	Limited pitch range (low)	Chapter 8, p. 160
The thin voice	Inadequate oral resonance	Chapter 5, p. 131
	Limited pitch range	Chapter 8, p. 160
	Poor breath control	Chapter 6, p. 143
	Insufficient use of gross abdominal muscles	Chapter 6, p. 141

* NOTE: For skill acquisition of rate control, review your work in Chapter 2. Check yourself for clarity of sounds. A book of simple poetry can be helpful in aiding you to vary your rate as it is related to meaning.

Page References for Voice Improvement in
Improving Voice and Articulation (continued)

Quality	Analysis	References
The throaty voice	Insufficient oral resonance	Chapter 5, p. 131
	Lax movement of articulators	Chapter 2
	Faulty emission of breath	Chapter 6, p. 147
	Possible physiological condition	See physician
The breathy voice	Possible physiological condition	See physician
	Hypolaryngeal tension	Chapter 7, p. 153
	Inadequate oral resonance	Chapter 5, p. 132
	Incorrect respiration	Chapter 6, p. 144
The husky voice	Same as above	
	Limited pitch range (low)	Chapter 8, p. 160
The harsh voice	Hyperlaryngeal tension	Chapter 7, p. 157
	Hyperpharyngeal resonance	Chapter 5, p. 128
	Overprojection, overenergizing	Chapter 6, p. 148
The hoarse voice	Possible temporary or chronic physiological condition	See physician
	Poor respiration habits	Chapter 6, p. 143
	Hyperlaryngeal tension	Chapter 7, p. 157
The nasal voice		
Hypernasality	Faulty use of velum	Chapter 5, p. 133
	Possible hypertension in resonators	Chapter 6, p. 128
Hyponasality	Faulty use of velum	Chapter 5, p. 133
	Lax articulators	Chapter 2
Assimilation Nasality	Misdirected resonance	Chapter 5, p. 135
	Incorrect use of velum	Chapter 5, p. 133
Glottal attacks	Hyperlaryngeal tension	Chapter 7, p. 157
	Faulty control of breath emission	Chapter 6, p. 143

Suggested Readings for Voice Improvement

The strident voice: Anderson, Virgil, A., *Training the Speaking Voice.* New York: Oxford University Press, 1961, (2d ed.) Chap. 3, pp. 75, 76.

Hahn, Elise, Loman, Charles W., Hargis, Donald E., and Vandragen, Daniel, *Basic Voice Training for Speech.* New York: McGraw-Hill Book Co., Inc., 1957 (2d ed.), Chap. 5, pp. 107–109.

The throaty voice: Hahn, Elise, Loman, Charles W., Hargis, Donald E., and Vandragen, Daniel, *Basic Voice Training for Speech.* New York: McGraw-Hill Book Co., Inc., 1957 (2d ed.), Chap. 5, pp. 107, 108.

Van Dusen, C. Raymond, *Training the Voice for Speech.* New York: McGraw-Hill Book Co., Inc., 1953, Chap. 13, pp. 137, 138.

The breathy voice: Anderson, Virgil A., *Training the Speaking Voice.* New York: Oxford University Press, 1961 (2d ed.), Chap. 3, pp. 68–72, pp. 93–96.

Hanley, Theodore D., and Thurman, Wayne L., *Developing Vocal Skills.* New York: Holt, Rinehart & Winston, 1962, Chap. 10, pp. 177–179.

The thin voice: Hanley, Theodore D., and Thurman, Wayne L., *Developing Vocal Skills.* New York: Holt, Rinehart & Winston, 1962, Chap. 10, pp. 179, 180.

Van Dusen, C. Raymond, *Training the Voice for Speech.* New York: McGraw-Hill Book Co., Inc., 1953, Chap. 13, pp. 138–140.

The harsh voice: Anderson, Virgil A., *Training the Speaking Voice.* New York: Oxford University Press, 1961 (2d ed.), Chap. 3, pp. 96–102.

Hahn, Elise, Loman, Charles W., Hargis, Donald E., and Vandragen, Daniel, *Basic Voice Training for Speech.* New York: McGraw-Hill Book Co., Inc., 1957, Chap. 5, p. 68, p. 72, p. 73, p. 74.

The hoarse voice: Anderson, Virgil A., *Training the Speaking Voice.* New York: Oxford University Press, 1961 (2d ed.), Chap. 3, pp. 72–74.

Hahn, Elise, Loman, Charles W., Hargis, Donald E., and Vandragen, Daniel, *Basic Voice Training for Speech.* New York: McGraw-Hill Book Co., Inc., 1957, Chap. 5, pp. 68–69.

The nasal voice: Anderson, Virgil A., *Training the Speaking Voice.* New York: Oxford University Press, 1961 (2d ed.), Chap. 4, pp. 128–143.
VanRiper, Charles, and Irwin, John V., *Voice and Articulation.* Englewood Cliffs, N.J.: Prentice-Hall, Inc., 1958, Chap. 8, pp. 239–251.

The denasal voice: Green, Margaret C. L., *The Voice and Its Disorders.* New York: The Macmillan Co., 1959, Chap. 13, pp. 147–152.
Hahn, Elise, Loman, Charles W., Hargis, Donald E., and Vandragen, Daniel, *Basic Voice Training for Speech.* New York: McGraw-Hill Book Co., Inc., 1957, Chap. 5, pp. 109–111.

Glottal attack: Eisenson, Jon, *The Improvement of Voice and Diction.* New York: The Macmillan Co., 1965 (2d ed.), Chap. 4, pp. 63–66.
Hahn, Elise, Loman, Charles W., Hargis, Donald E., and Vandragen, Daniel, *Basic Voice Training for Speech.* New York: McGraw-Hill Book Co., Inc., 1957, Chap. 5, pp. 67–68, pp. 71–72.

General: Green, Margaret C. L., *The Voice and Its Disorders.* New York: The Macmillan Co., 1959, Chap. 9, "Rehabilitation of the Patient with Vocal Strain," and Chap. 10, "Training in Voice Production."
Traves, Lee Edward (ed.), *Handbook of Speech Pathology.* New York: Appleton-Century-Crofts, Inc., 1957, Chap. 22, "Voice Disorders Associated with Organic Abnormalities," by Paul Moore.

Articulation Analysis Form

Consonants		Vowels	
Evaluation	*Comments*	*Evaluation*	*Comments*

Consonants Evaluation		Comments	Vowels Evaluation	Comments
p____	b____		i____	
t____	d____		ɪ____	
k____	g____		ɛ____	
l____	r____		æ____	
m____	n____		ɑ____	
ŋ____			ɒ____	
f____	v____		ɔ____	
θ____	ð____		ʊ____	
s____	z____		u____	
ʃ____	ʒ____		ʌ____	
ʍ____	w____		ə____	
h____			ɝ____	
j____			ɚ____	

Affricates	Diphthongs
tʃ____	eɪ____
dʒ____	aɪ____
	ɔɪ____
	oʊ____
	aʊ____

Specific Articulation Problems

Omissions

Additions

Substitutions and distortions

Transpositions

Consonant combinations

Consonant clusters

Incorrect syllabic stress

Overassimilation

Pedantic precision

Stressed form words

Voice Analysis Form

(Terms defined according to this handbook)

Evaluations   *Comments*

Vocal quality

Laryngeal function

Breathy_____

Husky_____

Strident_____

Raspy_____

Throaty_____

Harsh_____

Glottal_____

Adequate_____

Resonance

Thin_____

Hypernasal_____

Hyponasal_____

Balanced_____

Pitch

Too-high range_____

Too-low range_____

Pitch patterns_____

Monotonous_____

Adequate_____

Other_____

Volume

Inadequate projection_____

Overprojection_____

Voice fading_____

Lack of meaningful variation_____

Adequate_____

Other_____

Rate

Too rapid_____

Too slow_____

Lack of meaningful variation_____

Adequate_____

Other_____